T0116292

CAMBRIDGE CLASSICAL STUDIES VI

General Editors

F. M. CORNFORD, D. S. ROBERTSON, F. E. ADCOCK

THE ARCHITECTURE OF THE INTELLIGIBLE UNIVERSE IN THE PHILOSOPHY OF PLOTINUS

THE ARCHITECTURE OF THE INTELLIGIBLE UNIVERSE IN THE PHILOSOPHY OF PLOTINUS

An Analytical and Historical Study

by

A. H. ARMSTRONG

CAMBRIDGE
AT THE UNIVERSITY PRESS
1940

CAMBRIDGE UNIVERSITY PRESS
Cambridge, New York, Melbourne, Madrid, Cape Town,
Singapore, São Paulo, Delhi, Mexico City

Cambridge University Press
The Edinburgh Building, Cambridge CB2 8RU, UK

Published in the United States of America by Cambridge University Press, New York

www.cambridge.org
Information on this title: www.cambridge.org/9781107656734

First published 1940
First paperback edition 2013

A catalogue record for this publication is available from the British Library

ISBN 978-1-107-65673-4 Paperback

CONTENTS

INTRODUCTION

THE TITLE of this essay, "The Architecture of the Intelligible Universe in the Philosophy of Plotinus", requires some explanation. By the Intelligible Universe I mean the whole cosmic order of the three hypostases, the One, Νοῦς, and Soul, as perceptible to the intellect. This I have tried to examine from the point of view of its structure. That is, I have tried to determine how the various levels in the hierarchy of reality according to Plotinus fit in with each other and with the whole, what is their nature and function in relation to the universal order. In doing this I have found it necessary to investigate the historical origins of many of Plotinus's concepts, to try to discover the traditional reasons which led him to give such a very distinctive outline and articulation to his picture of reality. There is, I think, no general presupposition or preconceived idea about the philosophy of Plotinus underlying this study except (*a*) that it is not, for historical reasons, a fully consistent philosophy; and (*b*) that Plotinus is not an anti-rationalist, but that he believes in the existence of an objective reality which is orderly and so accessible to the human intellect. These beliefs I have tried to justify in my detailed examination.

My obligations both to persons and books are many. I have received much most valued help and encouragement from Professors F. M. Cornford and E. R. Dodds. In those passages in which I deal with Albinus and Numenius I am greatly indebted to Dr Ph. E. Merlan of Vienna, and in those dealing with the Stoics to Professor B. Farrington of Swansea. I give a short list of books which I have found relevant and helpful.

I. GENERAL HISTORIES OF PHILOSOPHY

BRÉHIER, E. *Histoire de la Philosophie*, I.
CAIRD, E. *Evolution of Theology in the Greek Philosophers.*
RITTER-PRELLER. *Historia Philosophiae Graecae.*
UEBERWEG-PRAECHTER. *Geschichte der Philosophie*, I. "Die Philosophie des Altertums", von K. Praechter.
ZELLER, E. *Die Philosophie der Griechen.*

II. PLATO

CORNFORD, F. M. *Plato's Theory of Knowledge.*
—— *Plato's Cosmology.*
GRUBE, G. M. A. *Plato's Thought.*
HARDIE, W. F. R. *A Study in Plato.*
ROBIN, L. *La Théorie Platonicienne des Idées et des Nombres.*
TAYLOR, A. E. *A Commentary on Plato's "Timaeus".*
—— *The "Parmenides" of Plato* (Oxford Translation).

III. ARISTOTLE

HICKS, R. D. Aristotle, *De Anima.*
ROSS, W. D. *Aristotle.*
—— Aristotle, *Metaphysics* (Introduction and Commentary).
—— Aristotle, *Physics* (Introduction and Commentary).

IV. THE EARLIER STOICS

BEVAN, E. *Stoics and Sceptics.*
BIDEZ, J. *Cité du Monde et Cité du Soleil chez les Stoïciens.*
BRÉHIER, E. *Chrysippe.*
HICKS, R. D. *Stoic and Epicurean.*

V. THE LATER STOICS. POSIDONIUS

DOBSON, J. F. "The Posidonius Myth", *C.Q.* 1918, p. 179.
JAEGER, W. *Nemesios von Emesa.*
REINHARDT, K. *Kosmos und Sympathie.*
—— *Poseidonios.*
THEILER, W. *Vorbereitung des Neu-Platonismus.*
WITT, R. E. "Plotinus and Posidonius", *C.Q.* vol. XXIV, 1930.

VI. THE MIDDLE PLATONISTS, NEO-PYTHAGOREANS, AND *HERMETICA*

SCOTT, W. *Hermetica* (3 vols. Introduction, Text and Commentary).
THEDINGA, Fr. *De Numenio Philosopho Platonico.*
WITT, R. E. *Albinus and the History of Middle Platonism.*

VII. THE LOGOS DOCTRINE

AALL, A. *Geschichte der Logos-Idee.*
HEINZE, R. *Die Lehre vom Logos.*

VIII. PHILO

BRÉHIER, E. *Les Idées Philosophiques et Religieuses de Philon.*
LEBRETON, J. *Histoire du Dogme de la Trinité*, vol. I (also for the Gnostics, vol. II).

IX. THE NEO-PLATONISTS

DODDS, E. R. *Proclus, The Elements of Theology* (Text, Translation, and Commentary).
WHITTAKER, T. *The Neo-Platonists.*

X. PLOTINUS

(*a*) Translation

MACKENNA, S. Plotinus, *The Enneads.*

(*b*) Translation with Notes and Appendices

BOUILLET, M. N. *Les Ennéades de Plotin.*

(*c*) Works on the philosophy of Plotinus

ARNOU, R. *Le Désir de Dieu dans la Philosophie de Plotin.*
BRÉHIER, E. *La Philosophie de Plotin.*
—— Introductions to the several treatises in the Budé edition of Plotinus.
DODDS, E. R. "The *Parmenides* of Plato and the Origin of the Neo-Platonic One", *C.Q.* vol. XXII, 1928, p. 129.
FULLER, B. A. G. *The Problem of Evil in Plotinus.*
HEINEMANN, F. *Plotin.*

HENRY, P. *Plotin et l'Occident.*
—— "Augustine and Plotinus", *Journal of Theological Studies*, vol. XXXVIII, Jan. 1937, No. 149.
INGE, W. R. *The Philosophy of Plotinus.*
NEBEL, G. *Plotins Kategorien der Intelligiblen Welt.*

I have tried to confine this list of books in the main to those which have a direct bearing on this essay. I have not included texts. For the *Enneads* I have used the Budé text except for the last four treatises of the Sixth Ennead, for which I have used Volkmann's Teubner edition.

A. H. A.

Section I. THE ONE

CHAPTER I

THE ONE. POSITIVE

GENERALIZATIONS about the philosophy of Plotinus are extremely dangerous. It seems, however, to be necessary to preface any attempt to analyse his views of the architecture of reality with some sort of comprehensive statement about their nature, however vague it may be and however much it may have to be qualified later. I have already tried to do this for the system as a whole in the Introduction.

In these first two chapters I proceed to a closer examination of the most baffling part of Plotinus's philosophy, his concept of the One. Plotinus's thought at this point is undoubtedly difficult, and not only, I think, because he is trying to express the inexpressible. This difficulty certainly exists for any philosopher who tries to penetrate the depths of being. In Plotinus, however, there is, I believe, as well, a real confusion of thought caused to a great extent by the complexity of the metaphysical tradition which he inherited. For this reason it is not possible to make any more definite statement about the One of Plotinus than that it is in his system the first and ultimate principle of reality. It would not be correct to call it without qualification the Absolute. This term really belongs to a philosophy of absolute and relative or necessary and contingent being, a philosophy in which Being is the primary concept and its analysis the most important task. Plotinus's system is not of this type. It would be more correct, too, to speak of "systems" than of a system. It is possible to derive from the *Enneads* several divergent and not completely reconcilable constructions of reality. These are not of course clearly separable. They blend into each other and intermix in a most disconcerting way. Any analysis, however careful and elaborate, is bound to lose something of the original. But in the interests of clear thinking it is desirable to make it. I propose, then, to consider some different ways in which Plotinus regards the One as head or first principle of the system of reality.

The first aspect of the One with which I propose to deal is that arrived at as the conclusion of the metaphysical and religious search for a First Cause, a ground of being, a self-sufficing source and director of all things, a primary reality which can act as an explanation of the universe. This line of thought does not seem at first as if it should lead Plotinus higher than his second hypostasis, Νοῦς. Νοῦς in his system can, and sometimes does, discharge all these functions in relation to the lower levels of being.[1] There is, at the same time, a strong tendency to transfer them to the One, a tendency for which, I think, reasons can be found even within the scope of this particular way of regarding it.

Νοῦς in Plotinus is the totality of being. That is, it is the organic world of Ideas, the objects of knowledge, and at the same time the mind that knows them. It is a perfect unity-in-duality of subject and object, the sphere in the macrocosm corresponding to the stage of perfect intuitive knowledge in the microcosm. It is the region of perfect knowledge in which, according to the Aristotelian psychology which deeply affected Plotinus, the mind becomes what it thinks.

Plotinus, however, insists that Νοῦς, even if it contains in itself the totality of being at one stage of its evolution, is not originative, is not the ultimate ground of reality. The Noetic world is a composite of Matter and Form, resulting from a double movement of withdrawal from and return to the One.[2] Or, again, it is the result of a multiplex contemplation of the Primal Unity.[3] With these aspects of the sphere of Νοῦς I shall deal more fully later. What I wish to stress here is its state of dependence on the One. This dependence persists even when, as in the eighth treatise of the Sixth Ennead, the One is described in terms almost identical with those applied to Νοῦς, or at least in language which suggests something more like Νοῦς than the unpredicable complete unity, the One-above-being,

[1] See Arnou, *Désir de Dieu*, p. 25, for Νοῦς as first principle in the rational intelligible order.

[2] II. 4. 5.

[3] VI. 7. 15.

of other passages. In VI. 8 the One is called pure will,[1] absolute ἐνέργεια,[2] love, and that love of Himself,[3] and the cause of Himself, and thus the cause of all that proceeds from Him, not merely the ground of all being in the sense of a primal element, but deliberately willing Himself and all that comes from Him. He is said to include all His effects.[4] This positive description of the One is very closely connected, especially in Ch. 18, with the light-metaphor of emanation[5] and the comparison of the One to the sun, a metaphor found throughout the *Enneads*.[6] It is obvious that this self-directed, self-loving God (I am using the terms of a later theology deliberately at this point), whose Being is Act directed upon His own perfection, from whom all other orders of being proceed as images of Him of varying degrees of adequacy, is not the mathematical Unity to which it is impossible to apply any predicate whatever. Plotinus may protest as much as he likes that he intends to introduce no sort of duality into the One, and that any appearance of duality which his words may suggest is due to the limitations of language. He takes the decisive step when he makes the One ἐνέργεια and gives it will, makes it eternally create itself and return eternally upon itself in love. This makes it inevitably an οὐσία, however much it may transcend the beings which we know, and if an οὐσία, then a one-in-many. It becomes a being to which predicates can be applied and about which logical distinctions can be made. The One-God can be regarded variously as lover, love, and loved, eternal creator, creative process, and eternally created, willer, will, and willed. This is necessary if the One is to be a First Cause in a system of Platonic-Aristotelian type. It must, in such a system, be a substance, however far it may transcend all substances known to us.[7] It must be the actuality which actualizes all potencies, and not itself a mere potentiality actualizing itself in the development of the universe. The One as bare unity, beyond being, could, strictly speaking, only be a "cause" in this latter sense.

1 Chs. 13, 21. 2 Cp. V. 6. 6. 3 Ch. 15.
4 Ch. 18. 5 See Ch. III.
6 I. 7. 1; V. 1. 2 and 10. 3. 12, 5. 7–8, 6. 4; VI. 9. 9.
7 Cp. V. 5. 13, especially the words εἴασε τὸ <u>ἔστιν</u> οὐδὲν καταμαρτυρήσας τῶν οὐ παρόντων.

Is it, then, still in any way possible to discover a real difference between Νοῦς and the One, even when all other ways of looking at the One are temporarily excluded? Νοῦς and the One are, from this point of view, unities and not-unities in the same sense,[1] beings possessed of self-intellection (denied elsewhere to the One) and self-concentration. There is really no need for the One here to be regarded as more than the aspect of Νοῦς which it presents when its unity rather than its diversity is stressed;[2] at least, so it appears at first. A real difference, however, remains.

To explain it, it is necessary to turn for a moment from drawing a metaphysical map of Plotinus's system and to consider it as a record of the spiritual life. It is clear enough from reading the *Enneads* that they are this, though they are also much more. It must be remembered that, for Plotinus, the frontier between microcosm and macrocosm is by no means rigid and precise. The boundaries shutting off the self from the universe are largely illusory, and disappear in the higher stages of perception.

Looked at in this way the distinction between Νοῦς and the One at its most Νοῦς-like becomes clear. Νοῦς is always the universal correlative to our highest mental state; it is the realm of νόησις, a realm well within our own human sphere. Plotinus draws a sharp distinction between soul and Νοῦς; but this does not affect man's status as inhabitant by nature of the intelligible world. In becoming "man", in discharging his functions in the lower world, man may cease to be the All; but on escaping from the lower world he resumes his higher status.[3] Plotinus often says that soul[4] or "man" is not Νοῦς. He does not often say that "we" are not Νοῦς. When he does say so[5] he soon qualifies his statement by returning to his

[1] See Nebel, *Plotins Kategorien der Intelligiblen Welt*, pp. 44–5, for the process of approximation by which Νοῦς through being considered primarily as a member of the "Hypostasenreihe" becomes less the Platonic World of Ideas and more a self-concentrated unity approximating closely to the One.

[2] See Nebel, p. 15, n. 3 (distinction between "morphische Einheit" and "unum transcendentale").

[3] v. 8. 7.

[4] Soul, however, can also be thought of as belonging to the world of Νοῦς, though on its lowest edge, cp. IV. 8. 7.

[5] v. 3. 3.

doctrine that we can become Νοῦς by ceasing to be "man".[1] The human being, in the totality of its realizable powers, is for Plotinus much more than soul. It is Νοῦς.

The One, on the other hand, whether considered in relation to the human or the universal mind, is normally thought of by Plotinus as something extra, something outside and beyond, which we can only attain by leaving ourselves behind.[2] It is that which is left over, which remains outside and transcending our systematization and classification of the cosmos. It is "light above light".[3] This is expressed strikingly in the seventh treatise of the Sixth Ennead, where the effluence from the Good is spoken of as a sort of "bloom" upon Νοῦς, a χάρις ἐπιθέουσα τῷ κάλλει.[4] Even its effects are something extra to the nature of Νοῦς, something, one might almost say, supernatural.

This character of the One is of peculiar interest because it is the first clear appearance in Greek philosophy of any conception of an Absolute, of a ground of being in some way different in kind from that of which it is the ground. Plotinus is by no means consistent in this conception. The One is always getting inside the cosmos, becoming part of the system. In fact the whole theory of necessary emanation is designed to bring it within the cosmos, to make it organically connected with the whole. It was this confusion which led to the later Neo-Platonic development through Iamblichus's super-One, which is not the Good, above Plotinus's One-Good[5] to the ἀπόρρητον of Damascius.[6] It also helps to mark the distinction between Plotinus and the Christian philosophers. There are also the passages to be taken into consideration where Plotinus regards Νοῦς as a stage in our full self-realization rather than its end and asserts the identity of the innermost or highest Self and the One.[7] This type of thought occurs throughout the *Enneads*, and will have to be discussed in detail later.[8] It may be said here, however, that at least the realization of identity with the One is for Plotinus a

[1] v. 3. 4. [2] iii. 8. 1; v. 4. 1. [3] v. 3. 12.
[4] vi. 7. 22; cp. vi. 7. 21 (the "other light") and 31.
[5] *Theol. Arith.* 1. *De Myst.* 8. 2.
[6] *Dubitationes et Solutiones de Primis Principiis*, 2–8.
[7] Cp. v. 1. 11; vi. 7. 36, 9. 11. [8] Ch. iii

temporary and abnormal state and that Νοῦς, the intelligible realm, is for him the normal home and most fully natural state of the human being in a way in which neither the One nor the visible universe is. If we confine ourselves for the moment to considering the "positive" aspect of the One as God discussed in this chapter we can safely say that it is distinguished from Νοῦς by its "supernatural" or "transcendent" as distinct from a "natural" or "normal" character. Νοῦς is certainly θεός, but the One comes much nearer to the Christian conception of God.

A second reason, of course, for the stressing of the transcendence of the One in VI. 8 and treatises of similar emphasis is that the aspect of the One which we have just been considering is never separated from the mathematical concept of the unity which generates plurality but is not itself multiple.[1] But before discussing this it will be desirable to consider the historical origin of the conception of the One as God, which appears so clearly in VI. 7 and 8. It is not a new conception of Plotinus. The beginnings of it appear in Plato, at least in Plato as understood by the Platonists of the early Roman Empire, with the mention of the "Idea of the Good" in *Republic*, VI. This single, highly metaphorical allusion, however, is not the real basis of the well worked-out description of the Supreme in, for instance, *Enneads*, VI. 8. Behind this stands the systematic theology of Aristotle. It is a striking example of the very great and perhaps not sufficiently realized influence of Aristotle upon Plotinus. There is a phrase in Porphyry's biography which it is important that the student of Plotinus should remember, καταπεπύκνωται δὲ (ἐν τοῖς συγγράμμασι) καὶ ἡ Μετὰ τὰ φυσικὰ τοῦ 'Αριστοτέλους πραγματεία.[2] This is not far from the truth. Not only the teaching of the *Metaphysics* but that of the *De Anima* is to be found firmly embedded in the *Enneads*. The resemblance in particular between VI. 8 and *Metaphysics* Λ is very striking. This transcendent self-sufficing God, pure and self-directed Act, the supreme object of desire, but himself desiring nothing but himself, appears in philosophy before Plotinus only in Aristotle, and in the Platonic literature of the Imperial period. The chief claim to distinction of Plotinus's

[1] VI. 8. 8, 9, 11, 17. [2] *Vita Plotini*, 14.

master, the mysterious Ammonius Saccas, was to have reconciled Plato and Aristotle, and in this he was following a well-established tradition. The philosophers who took part in this Platonic-Pythagorean revival not only try to reconcile Plato and Aristotle but at times seem to be quite unconscious that Aristotle's teachings are not Platonic. There was, of course, also an anti-Aristotelian tradition of Platonism, of which the chief exponent is Atticus. The violence of his polemic against Aristotle and the Aristotelianizing of Plato is a witness to the strength with which the opposing view was held. It is interesting to note that, in spite of his affectation of Platonic purity, Atticus himself is strongly influenced by Stoicism. Another testimony is furnished by Numenius's statement[1] that he found it necessary to separate Plato from Aristotle, as well as from Zeno and the Academy.

The two most notable representatives of these Aristotelianizing Platonists are Numenius himself and Albinus, the author of the *Didaskalikos*. This latter is an extraordinary work, claiming to be an account of the teachings of Plato, but at least half composed of doctrines taken unchanged and undigested from Aristotle, the Stoics, and other sources.[2] The author annexes, for example, without explanation or apology, Aristotle's whole system of formal logic.

The peculiar interest of these two, for the present purpose, is their treatment of Aristotle's conception of the supreme god as self-thinking mind. This they take over from the *Metaphysics* and identify, not with the Plotinian νοῦς, on the same level as the νοητά, but with the source or cause of the Ideas, the Platonic Idea of the Good. Numenius speaks of the Good as αὐτὸ δὲ ἐν εἰρήνῃ, ἐν εὐμενείᾳ, τὸ ἤρεμον, τὸ ἡγεμονικόν, ἵλεων ἐποχούμενον ἐπὶ τῇ οὐσίᾳ.[3] The resemblance here to Plotinus's One is striking. But he also says[4] ὁ νοῦς...μόνος εὕρηται ὢν τὸ ἀγαθόν,...ἀρκεῖ τὸ ἀγαθὸν οὐσίας

[1] Περὶ τῆς τῶν ᾿Ακαδημαϊκῶν πρὸς Πλάτωνα διαστάσεως. I. 8 in Thedinga's arrangement of the fragments.

[2] See R. E. Witt, *Albinus and the History of Middle Platonism*, for a full and most valuable discussion of this writer.

[3] Περὶ τἀγαθοῦ. I. 10, Thedinga.

[4] V. 25.

εἶναι ἀρχή, and εἰ δ' ἐστὶ μὲν νοητὸν ἡ οὐσία καὶ ἡ ἰδέα, ταύτης δ' ὡμολογήθη πρεσβύτερον καὶ αἴτιον εἶναι ὁ νοῦς. From this it is clear that this Good, source of being and the Ideas, is nothing else than Νοῦς. Of this Νοῦς or First God of the three gods he recognizes, this Demiourgos of being,[1] he says[2] ὁ θεὸς ὁ μὲν πρῶτος ἐν ἑαυτῷ ὢν ἐστιν ἁπλοῦς, διὰ τὸ ἑαυτῷ συγγιγνόμενος διόλου μή ποτε εἶναι διαιρετός...(30) ὁ μὲν πρῶτος θεὸς ἔσται ἑστώς, and ἀντὶ γὰρ τῆς προσούσης τῷ δευτέρῳ κινήσεως, τὴν προσοῦσαν τῷ πρώτῳ στάσιν φημὶ εἶναι κίνησιν σύμφυτον. Here we have clearly a link between Aristotle's God and the One of Plotinus. We have an attempt to put the Aristotelian self-sufficient and therefore eternally stable Νοῦς, with no movement directed to anything outside itself, at the head of the Platonic hierarchy of being. It has, however, to be admitted that Numenius does not seem to have been quite consistent in putting his First God above the Ideas. The phrase ὁ μὲν οὖν πρῶτος περὶ τὰ νοητά, ὁ δὲ δεύτερος περὶ τὰ νοητὰ καὶ αἰσθητά[3] may only mean that the First makes the νοητά. It is difficult, however, to accept this interpretation, as the Second God cannot be thought of as employed in making the Ideas; though Numenius says[4] ὁ γὰρ δεύτερος διττὸς ὢν αὐτοποιεῖ[5] τήν τε ἰδέαν ἑαυτοῦ καὶ τὸν κόσμον, in spite of the statement (34) that the Πρῶτος Νοῦς, the αὐτοαγαθόν, is the ἰδέα of the Demiourgos or Second God. This puzzle is perhaps cleared up by the words immediately following in fr. 25 ἔπειτα θεωρητικὸς ὅλως,[6] taken in connection with the statement of Proclus[7] that Numenius represents the First taking the Second Νοῦς into partnership in its activity of νόησις. According to this interpretation the Idea of himself which the Demiurge or Second God creates would be the reflection of the αὐτοαγαθόν in his own contemplative mind, an immanent form derived from the First God. We thus find in Numenius two orders of Ideal Being corresponding to the First and Second Gods, the two grades of οὐσία referred

[1] v. 25. [2] v. 26, 30. [3] v. 30. [4] 25.

[5] αὐτὸ ποιεῖ E: αὐτοποιεῖ Thed. αὐτὸς...cet. αὐτός is perhaps the better reading. Proximity of αὐτὸ ἀγαθόν might account for αὐτὸποιεῖ.

[6] ἔπειτα here however seems to have no acceptable meaning. Professor Dodds suggests ὁ δ' ἐπέκεινα θεωρητικὸς ὅλως, which agrees with the doctrine of the other fragments.

[7] *In Tim.* III. 103.

to[1] as μία μὲν ἡ τοῦ πρώτου, ἑτέρα δὲ ἡ τοῦ δευτέρου. What, then, is exactly the relation of each of these grades to its appropriate Νοῦς, and what becomes of the exaltation of the First Νοῦς above the Ideas? In another fragment[2] Numenius, Proclus says, τὸν μὲν πρῶτον κατὰ τὸ ὅ ἐστι ζῷον τάττει (τὸ ὅ ἐστι ζῷον being the Ideal world of the *Timaeus*[3]). This, taken in conjunction with fr. 30, suggests a relationship between Νοῦς, even the πρῶτος νοῦς, and the Ideas more like that in Plotinus, thought and object of thought co-equal and co-eternal, rather than one of producer and product.

It seems however best to suppose that, as in the *Didaskalikos*, Νοῦς is thought of as prior to and the cause of its thoughts or objects of thought, the νοητά or Ideal World. Plotinus's doctrine of the co-equality and reciprocal action of thinker and thought,[4] derived from Aristotle's psychology, does not yet appear. This fits in well with the statement that the Second God *makes* his own Idea. The whole system arises from an attempt to interpret the *Timaeus* in a manner consistent with Aristotle.

The explanation of the statement that the Second Νοῦς is περὶ τὰ νοητὰ καὶ αἰσθητά is to be found in fr. 26, where the sphere of the Second is said to extend into ὕλη; it not only unifies ὕλη but is pluralized by it, in the process of thinking αἰσθητά.

In Numenius's system, then, we have at the head an Aristotelian Νοῦς-θεός, not concerned with actual creation[5] but only with himself, radiating τὰ θεῖα[6] as an incident or consequence of his self-contemplation, as in Plotinus, and so the Demiourgos of Being.[7] The soul is said ὁμιλῆσαι τῷ ἀγαθῷ μόνῳ μόνον.[8]

[1] Fr. 25.

[2] 39. Thedinga in this fragment inserts a πρῶτον without MS authority, which gives an absurd meaning contradicting everything else which we know of Numenius. If we read τὸν ⟨νοοῦντα⟩ νοῦν, as Dodds suggests, there is no inconsistency.

[3] Cp. *Enn.* II. 9. 6; V. 9. 9.

[4] Even in Plotinus Νοῦς sometimes seems to be in effect prior to the νοητά; cp. Nebel, pp. 44–5, and below Ch. V.

[5] 27.

[6] 29.

[7] According to Thedinga's reading at the end of fr. 10 this First νοῦς or αὐτοαγαθόν is called τὸ ἕν. This is possible in view of Numenius's Pythagorean preoccupations and is supported by fr. 14 (Chalc. *in Tim.* 293–7). It is not, however, in the best MSS.

[8] Cp. φυγὴ μόνου πρὸς μόνον. *Enn.* VI. 9, last words.

Albinus in his *Didaskalikos* is even more interesting. In his tenth chapter he combines elements of the discussion of the One in the *Parmenides*,[1] *Republic* VI, the Second Letter of Plato[2] and the theology of Aristotle's *Metaphysics*. The following passage from this chapter is worth quoting at length:

"Since Intellect is superior to Soul, and the Intellect in Act which thinks all things simultaneously and perpetually is superior to the Intellect in potency, and the cause of this and whatever may be still higher than these is fairer than this; this would be the First God, being the cause of perpetual actuality (τοῦ ἀεὶ ἐνεργεῖν) to the Intellect of the whole heaven. It acts towards this, being itself unmoved, as the sun towards seeing, whenever it looks upon it, and as the desired object, remaining unmoved, moves the desire. Thus this Intellect moves the Intellect of the whole heaven. But since the First Intellect is the most fair, it must have the fairest object of thought. But nothing is fairer than itself. It will, therefore, always think itself and its own thoughts, and its Actuality is its Idea (καὶ αὕτη ἡ ἐνέργεια αὐτοῦ ἰδέα ὑπάρχει)."

He continues by calling this First Νοῦς ἀγαθόν, καλόν, σύμμετρον, ἀλήθεια, πατήρ. He then proceeds to the section deriving from the First Hypothesis of the *Parmenides*. In this he says that the First Νοῦς is *not* genus, species (or form), differentia, accident (again Aristotelian terminology), evil, good, with or without quality, part, whole, does not move, is not moved, is not the same or other. About this "negative theology" I shall have more to say later.

Here again, just as in Numenius, we have a system professing to be Platonic but headed by the Aristotelian God. In the passage quoted above it appears even more Aristotelian than that of Numenius, for the Ideas are not mentioned, and next to the supreme Mind there appears the Mind of the whole Heaven. Also the Mind in potency and ὁ πάντα νοῶν καὶ ἅμα καὶ ἀεί certainly come from Aristotle's psychology. The position of the Ideas, however, has been defined in the previous chapter, 9. ἔστι δὲ ἡ ἰδέα ὡς μὲν πρὸς θεὸν νόησις αὐτοῦ, ὡς δὲ πρὸς ἡμᾶς νοητὸν πρῶτον, ὡς δὲ πρὸς τὴν

[1] See below Ch. II.

[2] 312E (the three Powers or Principles).

ὕλην μέτρον, ὡς δὲ πρὸς τὸν αἰσθητὸν κόσμον παράδειγμα, ὡς δὲ πρὸς αὑτὴν ἐξεταζομένη οὐσία. That is, they are the "thoughts of God" of Ch. 10. Their relation to the Mind of the whole Heaven is not clear. The difference, however, between the First and this Second Mind is clearly that the former thinks itself, is self-contained and self-directed, while the latter is directed to the First as to something external. The First Mind seems to create and contain the Ideas as νοήματα. The Mind of the Heaven is directed to this complex of νοῦς-νοήματα. We thus get an Aristotelian elaboration of the *Timaeus* influenced by *Republic* VI with its suggestion of the derivation of the Ideal World from a higher principle, by the mysterious later number-Platonism developed by Speusippus, and by the Monad-Νοῦς-God of Xenocrates.[1] The νοῦς-νοήματα is equivalent to the Absolute Living Creature, the World of Ideas in the *Timaeus*, the Mind of the Heaven to the Demiurge. There is no real attempt to relate the Aristotelian conception of the First Mind to its description by negation as an unpredicable unity in terms of the *Parmenides*.

One point about the system which does emerge fairly clearly is that we have here a God who, though he is still Νοῦς, ranks above ὁ νοῦς κατ' ἐνέργειαν πάντα νοῶν καὶ ἅμα καὶ ἀεί. In Numenius the situation is analogous. We have then in this "Platonism" of the second century A.D. a division of the spiritual, actual world into two parts, both eternal and unchanging but one self-contained, self-sufficient, uncaused or self-caused, and the other derived, not in itself sufficient for itself but deriving its being and activity from an eternal movement of contemplation and desire towards the First. This division, this conception of a First Principle higher than the active Mind-Demiurge which produces the world of the senses, has been arrived at by the conflation of the αὐτὸ τὸ ἀγαθόν with the νοῦς-θεός of Aristotle. The complete transcendence of Aristotle's God, its entire severance from the world and enclosure in its own activity of self-thinking is probably the origin of the very strongly-marked severance between the First God and the Demiurge.[2]

[1] Fr. 15; Witt, *Albinus*, pp. 16–17.

[2] Albinus's description of his First Principle (in Ch. X of the *Didaskalikos*) as Transcendent Cause in language which develops Plato's image

Numenius's statement that the First may not δημιουργεῖν and is ἀργὸν ἔργων ξυμπάντων, though it can be paralleled from Philo Judaeus, is probably Aristotelian rather than Oriental in its origin. The fusion of Aristotle's and Plato's first principles was probably greatly helped by Xenocrates's doctrine of the Νοῦς-Monad, which certainly influenced Albinus.[1] The Middle Platonist conception of Νοῦς, however, derives from Aristotle rather than Xenocrates. It is obvious that here we have a source of the utmost importance for Plotinus's doctrine of the One. In his conception of a First Principle and ground of existence higher than Νοῦς and the Ideas he is, as it has now become clear, not original but stands at the end of a tradition of which the dominant feature is the assimilation of Plato and Aristotle. There is little trace at this point in the system of Orientalism or the introduction from foreign sources of doctrines strange to the Greek tradition. The One as supreme source of being[2] is really Aristotle's God carried to a yet higher degree of remoteness by identification with the αὐτὸ τὸ ἀγαθόν, and by the same identification brought into relation with the νοητά. Intertwined with this conception in the *Didaskalikos* we have found traces of a "negative theology", based on an interpretation of the *Parmenides* which makes the First Principle an unpredicable logical unity. The immediate source, then, of the main elements in Plotinus's doctrine of the One is clear.

Before going on to consider the second aspect of the One, that in which it is considered as a unity beyond all definition or predication, I must mention a notable difference between Aristotle's θεός and the One of Plotinus even in its most Aristotelian aspect. Aristotle's God is a self-thinking mind; this is the essence of the conception. In Plotinus,[3] on the other hand, though there is the same self-direction, the same self-sufficiency, the same implicit logical duality of subject and object, the One does not only think itself, it wills and loves itself. This may partly be accounted for by the fact that this

of the Sun in Republic VI–VII shows another historical reason for this stressing of transcendence and an important source for the "negative theology of positive transcendence" discussed in my third chapter.

[1] Witt, *l.c.*

[2] See I. 6; V. I (especially Chs. 6 and 7) and VI. 8.

[3] VI. 8. 16.

particular treatise is concerned primarily with the question of free will. Plotinus also possibly was conscious that the unity produced by self-willing and self-loving was closer and had in it less of the duality he was trying to escape than that produced by self-directed knowledge. The lover and beloved are united more completely than thought and object of thought.[1]

This idea appears again in St Thomas Aquinas. St Thomas conceives of knowledge in the manner of Aristotle as a unitive act, tending towards the identification of knower and known. This unitive act, however, can only attain to its completion if knowledge engenders and passes over into love. "Filius autem est verbum non qualecunque, sed spirans amorem....Non igitur secundum quam libet perfectionem intellectus mittitur Filius, sed secundum talem instructionem intellectus, qua prorumpat in affectionem amoris."[2]

[1] I cannot accept the interpretation of this chapter given by E. Benz, *Marius Victorinus*, pp. 290 ff.: according to which we have here a "Selbsthypostasierung des Geistes in der Selbstschau" which is *substituted* for the normal doctrine of the Three Hypostases. There is no close parallel here to the Christian doctrine of the Holy Trinity. See Theiler in *Gnomon*, vol. x, pp. 497–9.

[2] St Thomas Aquinas, *Summa Theologica*, I. 43, cp. *Enn.* VI. 7. 35 (of the relation of Νοῦς to the One).

CHAPTER II

THE ONE. NEGATIVE

THE aspect of the One which I next propose to consider, that in which it presents itself as an unpredicable unity, is very closely connected with that just discussed. The two occur inextricably intertwined throughout the *Enneads*. In the earliest period, certainly, the aspect of the One as God, or active First Cause, is certainly that most stressed;[1] but later on, as in v. 1 and vi. 8, the two concepts run side by side. Plotinus's thought on the whole shows remarkably little trace of change or development throughout the *Enneads*; which is not very remarkable, as his writings were all produced within a comparatively short space of time at the end of his life.

We have already found both aspects side by side in Albinus, well established, that is, already in the Platonic tradition, very Hellenic and very much of the schools, which Plotinus inherited. The two have their point of contact in the straining after an absolute simplicity in the Divine nature characteristic of all Greek philosophy, for which composition implied dissolubility.

The "negative" way of regarding the One may be thought of as a specifically Pythagorean development of Platonism as a philosophy of numbers. The One has not only become very much more remote. Plotinus's conception of it is, in this aspect, limited by archaic mathematical logical considerations. It is unity itself, indivisible even in thought, and therefore unpredicable and indeed unthinkable. It is not-Being, not in the sense that it transcends all beings knowable to us, but because being simply cannot be predicated of it because it refuses all predication. Of course the positive and negative aspects of the One are never clearly separated in the *Enneads*. They are for Plotinus no more than slightly different ways of looking at the complex concept of a primal unity

[1] See below, pp. 23 ff.

and ground of being. It is when we come to trace their historical origins that we first see them clearly as essentially different ways of thinking about the First Principle. We can then see how the "negative" tradition led Plotinus into making negations about the One which are not required by the conception of positive transcendence.

In tracing the historical origins of this conception I am only trying to work out in greater detail the suggestions of Professor Dodds in his article "The Parmenides of Plato and the Neo-Platonic One".[1]

In this negative conception of the One it is spoken of as οὐδέν,[2] ἄμορφον, ἀνείδεον πρὸ εἴδους παντὸς,[3] μηδὲ τὸ ἐκεῖνο μηδὲ τὸ τοῦτο.[4] This conception can be traced back, as I have already suggested, and as Professor Dodds shows conclusively, to an interpretation of Plato's *Parmenides*. How close the language used in that dialogue about τὸ ἕν of the First Hypothesis is to that used by Plotinus about his First Principle will be shown by comparing the sets of parallel passages given by Dodds.[5]

The question of the real meaning of the second part of the *Parmenides* is irrelevant to this discussion. It seems fairly probable that it was intended as a preparation for the discussion of the interpenetrability of the μέγιστα γένη in the *Sophist* and a demonstration that if being, unity, etc., are mutually exclusive, then dialectic becomes impossible.[6] In any case it is pretty certain that Plato was not indulging in any Neo-Platonic speculations about the One.[7]

1 *C.Q.* vol. XXII. 1928, 3, p. 129.

2 VI. 9. 5.

3 VI. 9. 3.

4 *Ib.*

5 *Parm.* 137D–E = *Enn.* V. 5. 11; 138A = V. 5. 9; 139B = VI. 9. 3; 139E = IV. 5. 1; 140B = V. 5. 6; 140D = V. 5. 4; 141A = VI. 9. 3; 141E = V. 4. 1, and VI. 7. 38; 142A = V. 3. 13 and V. 3. 14.

6 Cornford, *Plato's Theory of Knowledge*, Introd. p. xii.

7 See the Appendix E, p. 145 to A. E. Taylor's Oxford translation of the *Parmenides* for a full discussion. A powerful defence of the Neo-Platonic interpretation of the *Parmenides* has been recently made by Mr W. F. R. Hardie in *A Study in Plato* (Oxford, 1936), especially in Ch. x, "The Enigma of the Parmenides", pp. 99–130. While not completely convinced by Mr Hardie's arguments, I think that there can be no doubt that he has established the claim of the Neo-Platonic exegesis to be taken seriously by modern scholars as a possible and legitimate way of under-

The intermediate stages by which the *Parmenides* was transformed into a source of Neo-Platonic doctrine are, however, of great interest and importance. Dodds bases his reconstruction of the tradition on two passages from Simplicius. The first, a citation from the Platonist Eudorus,[1] states that the Pythagoreans posited a ἓν ἀρχὴ τῶν πάντων which was prior to the ἓν τὸ τῇ δυάδι ἀντικείμενον. The first One is called ἀρχή, the second and the Indeterminate Dyad στοιχεῖα. This is confirmed by Proclus[2] who says that "as the Pythagoreans say, the One is prior to all oppositeness". Syrianus, also, attributes to the rather mythical Pythagorean Brotinus the statement that ἡ ἑνιαία αἰτία...νοῦ παντὸς καὶ οὐσίας δυνάμει καὶ πρεσβείᾳ ὑπερέχει. Here we have the One which is before mathematical number and its elements spoken of in the same terms as Plato's Idea of the Good and the transcendent Mind-above-Mind of Numenius and Albinus. Albinus too, we remember, applied to his First Principle in the tenth chapter of his treatise the negations of the First Hypothesis of the *Parmenides*.[3] Dodds's second passage from Simplicius[4] brings this tradition into still closer connection with the *Parmenides*. He has demonstrated fairly certainly that it goes back

standing the dialogue. My reasons for not being completely convinced, stated very shortly, are (i) Mr Hardie's explanation (p. 116) of the passage in 142 A, where it is flatly denied that the conclusions of the First Hypothesis can be true of the One, seems to go beyond anything that can be got out of the text. (ii) It is difficult to bring the *Parmenides* so interpreted into any connection with the line of thought adopted in the *Sophist*. (iii) The other evidence for anything like the Neo-Platonic One in Plato does not for the most part seem to suggest anything more than a One-Being (this would apply also to Eucleides in Diog. Laert. II. 106). This would seem to be confirmed by the later tradition, and notably by Xenocrates's Νοῦς-Monad. Only the Good ἐπέκεινα τῆς οὐσίας in the *Republic* suggests the transcendent One of Plotinus, and I still think that this passage is too vague and isolated to support any definite conclusion.

[1] About 25 B.C. Simplicius *in Phys.* 181. 10–30. [2] *In Tim.* 54 D.

[3] It must be remembered, however, that Albinus regards the *Parmenides* simply as a logical exercise, not as containing any profound metaphysical teaching (*Didaskalikos* 6). He must, therefore, be held to be unconscious of the source of his "negative theology". (Cp. Klibansky, "Ein Proklos-Fund", *Sitzber. Heidelberg. Akad. d. Wiss.* 1928–9, p. 7.)

[4] *In Phys.* A, 7. 230. 34 ff., Diels.

to Moderatus (a Pythagorean of the first century A.D.) and contains a Neo-Pythagorean interpretation of Plato. In it we hear of three Ones, of which the first is ὑπὲρ τὸ εἶναι καὶ πᾶσαν οὐσίαν, the second ὄντως ὂν and τὰ εἴδη, while the third, τὸ ψυχικόν, is said to μετέχειν τοῦ ἑνὸς καὶ τῶν εἰδῶν. This is obviously an interpretation of the first three hypotheses of the *Parmenides*, if of anything in Plato. It corresponds with the Neo-Platonic exegesis of the dialogue given by Proclus, and is also found in Plotinus.[1] In this passage of Simplicius we find it going back to a Neo-Pythagorean well before Plotinus. We have also discovered that the idea which influenced this interpretation and was assisted by it in its development, the idea of a pure unity prior to all duality, source of the elements of number and all reality, goes back at least to before Eudorus. Dodds traces it as far back as Speusippus. Speusippus's first principle was certainly the One, as far as we can be certain of anything in his system. According to Aetius[2] he distinguished this One from Νοῦς. According to Aristotle's remarks on his system,[3] the best evidence about him which we possess, he made his One non-existent and compared it to a seed. He made it, also, the first of a series of ἀρχαί,[4] "one of numbers, one of magnitudes, finally one of soul". So far Speusippus sounds very Neo-Platonic; but there is one striking feature about his thought which differentiates it very sharply from the rest of the Platonic tradition, and makes it clear that he is not simply to be classed as a Pythagorean predecessor of Plotinus who puts the numbers in the place of the Ideas. In the passages cited from *Metaphysics* Λ and N Aristotle reiterates the statement that for Speusippus the more perfect came from the less, from the indefinite and incomplete. Perfection for him stood at the end of the process, not at the beginning. His One was indefinite and a seed in the sense that it was, to use Aristotelian language, a potentiality from which all subsequent actuality develops. Plotinus certainly calls his One Nothing, and says that it is formless; and it is difficult, as Heinemann says, to distinguish sometimes between the

[1] v. 1. 8.
[2] Ap. Stob. *Ecl.* 1. 29.
[3] *Met.* Z, 2. 1028b. 21; Λ, 7. 1072b. 30; N, 4. 1091a. 35, 5. 1092a. 11–15.
[4] Z, *l.c.*

characteristics of the One and of ὕλη in his system. There can, however, be no doubt that Plotinus would not for a moment have tolerated any confusion between them. He would never allow his One to be thought of as simply a potentiality, as lower in the scale of perfection than Νοῦς or Soul.

Speusippus's ideas make a curious break in the Platonic tradition. For Plato before him and Aristotle after him the Good, perfection, is at least logically prior to the imperfect, to that which is developing. This innovation by Speusippus may well have been one of the reasons why Aristotle left the Academy. It did not exercise any great direct influence on the later Platonic-Pythagorean tradition, deeply influenced as it was by the thought of Aristotle. Numenius, Albinus, and Plotinus are all clear that Act precedes Potency, that the Good and the Perfect stand at the beginning of the cosmic process and are not its ultimate result. Even Eudorus[1] speaks of his primal One as ὑπεράνω θεός, a term which could not be applied to the One of Speusippus, which has no religious or moral significance and cannot in any way be equated with God or the Good. What Speusippus did effect was the formulation of the characteristic "negative theology" of the tradition in Pythagorean mathematical terms. He was at least partly responsible for the idea of the transcendent First Cause as a strict and absolute Unity and therefore unthinkable and unpredicable, which has such curious and confusing results.

In spite of the inadequacy of our material, we can make a fairly probable guess at the origin of Speusippus's peculiar doctrine of the One. Aristotle[2] couples "the Pythagoreans" with Speusippus as holding it. This seems confirmed by what we know of the Pythagorean teaching about the Tetractys. It is always the Decad, the final number of the series, which is spoken of as perfect, divine, containing all things in itself. The Tetractys or Decad, the fullness of number, seems to have been the focus of a positively religious veneration.[3] The primal Monad, the originative principle, does not seem to have been regarded in the same way. It does not appear to

[1] Simplicius, *in Phys.* 36, 181. [2] *Met.* Λ, *l.c.*

[3] Philolaus ap. Stob. *Ecl.* I. 8, Diels, fr. 11; Aristotle, *Met.* A, 5. 986a. 8; Theo Smyrn. II. 49, pp. 106, 107, Hiller; *Theol. Arith.* 10. 60.

have been thought of as anything more than a source or origin. It is doubtful whether any of the few passages[1] where the Pythagorean Monad is said to be God or the Good represent genuine pre-Platonic Pythagorean teaching. Philo in a highly suspicious-looking passage[2] asserts that Philolaus professed belief in One God, but even so does not identify that God with the primal Monad.

The question now arises whether we can find in Plato, in his latest "Pythagoreanizing" period, any trace of a doctrine of a Primal One. There is certainly no suggestion of any such thing in the dialogues.[3] If, following Jackson,[4] we force the meaning of *Philebus*, 23C–27C, into conformity with what Aristotle says about the generation of the Ideas from the One and the Indefinite Dyad, by putting the Ideas in the *Philebus* into the "mixed" class, then we can get a hint of such a doctrine. The objections to such an interpretation, however, seem to me insuperable. Nor does the statement preserved by Aristoxenus,[5] before quoted, ἀγαθόν ἐστιν ἕν, help us much. It need mean no more than *Philebus*, 16D, where it is made clear that every Idea is a ἕν. We are left, then, with Aristotle's evidence.[6] The first passage, from *Metaphysics* A, tells us that the One is substance, not a mere predicate of something else, and that it is the formal or substantive cause of the Ideas, with "the great and

[1] Eudorus in Simplicius, *l.c.* Hippol. *Ref.* I. 2. Aet. I. 7. 18. For the opposite view on these last two passages see Gilbert, *Arch. Gesch. Phil.* XXII, 155.

[2] *Mund. Opif.* 33. R. Scoon, *Greek Philosophy before Plato*, p. 150, maintains the genuineness of the Philo-fragment. On pp. 141–50 he discusses the relationship of Philolaus's religious god to the power of Number supremely exemplified in the Decad.

[3] The passages in the *Epistles*, II. 312E and VI. 323C–D, with which Plotinus supports the Neo-Platonic interpretation of the *Parmenides* (V. I. 3) are not helpful to anyone without the Neo-Platonic confidence in unhistorical interpretation. See Taylor's *Parmenides*, App. E, pp. 146 ff.

[4] *Journal of Philology*, X. 253–98. See App. IV, p. 301 of G. M. A. Grube's *Plato's Thought*.

[5] *Harm. Elem.* II. 30, and Ross, *Metaphysics*. Commentary on A. 6. 987b. 12, vol. I, pp. 163 ff.

[6] *Met.* A, 6. 987b. 20 ff.; N, 1091b. 13.

the small" as matter. The second passage is at first sight a good deal more startling. It runs τῶν δὲ τὰς ἀκινήτους οὐσίας εἶναι λεγόντων οἱ μέν φασιν αὐτὸ τὸ ἓν τὸ ἀγαθὸν αὐτὸ εἶναι οὐσίαν μέντοι τὸ ἓν αὐτοῦ ᾤοντο εἶναι μάλιστα. οἱ μέν... are presumably the conservative Platonists, notably Xenocrates, and Plato himself. The statement that for them the One Itself was the Good Itself seems almost too Neo-Platonic to be true. When we consider it a little more closely, however, we see that, as far as our evidence goes, we are dealing with a doctrine entirely different from anything in Plotinus. To begin with, the One in both the passages just quoted is an οὐσία. It is true that the Good Itself in *Republic* VI is said to be ἐπέκεινα τῆς οὐσίας, but this passage is so curiously isolated and seems so detached from the rest of Plato's thought that it is dangerous to argue from it that for Plato the good must always be beyond being. Surely if he had asserted that his One-Good was ἐπέκεινα τῆς οὐσίας Aristotle would have recorded the statement, however far from understanding its meaning he might have been. Further, the supreme Monad of Xenocrates, which he called Zeus and even Νοῦς,[1] was certainly not beyond being. What Plato seems to have meant by the identification of the One with the Good, and in general by the identification of the Ideas with numbers,[2] was that the Ideas were best expressed mathematically, that what made the Idea what it was, gave it, or rather was, its distinctive quality or individuality, was its number or "mathematical formula". This seems to be suggested by the identification in the *Philebus*[3] of the principle of definiteness with number and is clearly implied by the "identification of numbers with things" attributed to Plato in the *De Anima*.[4] Thus the widest Idea, the Good, in which all the others participate, and which is in some sense their cause, is equivalent to and represented by the primal number, One. There is, however, no evidence at all that this One-Good was regarded by Plato as possessing the negative characteristics of Unity-Absolute, of the non-existent One of the *Parmenides*.

[1] Fr. 15; Stob. *Ecl.* I. 62.

[2] I adopt Ross's view (Introduction to his edition of the *Metaphysics*, pp. lxvii–lxxi) rather than that of Robin (*La Théorie Platonicienne des Idées et des Nombres*, pp. 454 ff.).

[3] 25.

[4] 404b. 18 ff.

If Cornford's view of the development of Plato's later thought as evidenced in the *Sophist*,[1] and of the relation of the *Parmenides* to this development is correct, as I think it is, it is impossible that he should have had any such idea. According to this interpretation the discussion in the *Sophist*[2] is concerned with the interpenetration and interrelation of the Ideas, and with the denial that unity, or being, or any other Idea exists in absolute isolation; and the *Parmenides* is simply a negative preparation for this conclusion, a demonstration of the absurdities which follow from its rejection. Another characteristic of the One of Plato and Xenocrates which differentiates it from the normal teaching of Plotinus, is its constant association, though in a superior position, with the Indefinite Dyad in the production of the Ideas. The Indefinite Dyad had a curious history, and she makes a very interesting appearance in the *Enneads*. I shall say more about her when I come to discuss Plotinus's theory of emanation with its variants and alternatives.

It seems, then, impossible to find a source for the "negative theology", for the extreme transcendence and absolute unity of the Plotinian One, in Plato or Xenocrates. What we do find is a positive doctrine of the One-Good, which in its later, Xenocratean form, when the Monad is identified with Νοῦς,[3] is, with Aristotle's theology, the basis of the Middle Platonist theological tradition,[4] and so of that aspect of Plotinus's thought described in the previous chapter. For the most distinctive characteristic of Neo-Platonic theology, the unknowable, negatively transcendent One, we do not seem able to go back beyond Speusippus. Even to go back so far presents a serious difficulty. Speusippus certainly made the One first of a series of ἀρχαί, of numbers, magnitudes, and soul.[5] He also, according to Aetius,[6] distinguished the One from νοῦς. He also may have asserted that his One was prior not only to the Good (which is

[1] F. M. Cornford, *Plato's Theory of Knowledge*, Introd. p. xii, and pp. 252 ff.

[2] 251 A ff.

[3] Stobaeus, *l.c.*

[4] There seems to be good reason for supposing an influence of Xenocrates on Albinus; see Witt, *Albinus*, Ch. III, pp. 14 ff.

[5] *Met.* Z, 2. *l.c.*

[6] Ap. Stob. *Ecl.* I. 58.

fairly certain) but to being, was not existent.[1] In him, if in any known Greek philosopher, is to be found the origin of the ideas which governed the interpretation of the *Parmenides* in terms of the "negative theology". The trouble is, that on the first appearances of this type of thought, in Eudorus and later in Moderatus, we find that the primal One, that which stands before the One which is partner of the Indefinite Dyad, is not only ἀνούσιον but ὑπερούσιον. It is ὑπὲρ τὸ εἶναι καὶ πᾶσαν οὐσίαν (Moderatus), ὑπεράνω θεός (Eudorus). Speusippus's One on the other hand may be ἀνούσιον, but from everything that Aristotle says about it, it is quite certain that it was not ὑπερούσιον. It did not transcend being, was not more but less than the Good. The distinguishing characteristic of his system is that it is evolutionary, that it proceeds from the imperfect to the perfect. He seems also, to judge from one passage in Aristotle,[2] not only to have rejected the Ideas in favour of mathematical number as the ultimate realities,[3] but to have done so because he disliked mixing his mathematics with theology and morality, and refused to make the Indefinite Dyad the principle of evil. There is no evidence, even, that he insisted on the absolute unity of his One and hence its unknowableness and unpredicability, though he may well have done so. In any case, between him and Eudorus the whole scale of values has been inverted. The transcendent One is now beyond the highest limit of the scale of reality instead of below its lowest. It is easy to see that this could have happened, in view of the existence of Xenocrates's doctrine of a positive One at the head of the hierarchy of being. The only alternative is to suppose that Eudorus is expounding a genuinely Pythagorean tradition in which the primal Monad was not only originative but supreme, and that it was from either Moderatus himself or an unknown earlier Pythagorean that the application of this tradition to the interpretation of the *Parmenides* originated. If we suppose this, there is no need to bring in Speusippus at all, and the Neo-Platonic One seems likely to

[1] *Met.* N, 5. 1042a. 15. There is reason to doubt whether this is Speusippus's own teaching or a conclusion drawn from his premises by Aristotle. See Ross's note on the passage.

[2] N, 1091b. 32.

[3] Λ, 1075b. 37; N, 1090b. 13.

go back to Pythagoras himself! It is, however, made unlikely by the presence of the Indefinite Dyad in the Eudorus passage for, as Dodds[1] points out, she is Platonic, not Pythagorean.[2] It is better to suppose a modification of Speusippus under the influence of the latest thought of Plato, Xenocrates and, perhaps most important of all, an interpretation of *Republic* VI, 509B (the Good "beyond being") similar to that attributed by Syrianus[3] to the Neo-Pythagorean pseudo-Brotinus.[4]

The later history of the doctrine is also rather curious. It seems to be dominant in the Neo-Pythagoreanism of Moderatus, but in Numenius, as well as in the Platonist Albinus, it has fallen into the background. Numenius is only made to speak of his supreme principle as τὸ ἕν in a reading in fr. 10, Thedinga, not found in the best MSS.[5] There is, however, no doubt that the supreme god or First principle in both these writers is a superior Νοῦς.[6] The change probably took place under the influence of Aristotle.[7] Albinus still retains in his tenth chapter a large undigested lump of "negative theology".[8] It is a discordant and alien element in his system. It is probable that it remained an undigested and alien element in the Platonic tradition till it reached Plotinus, to whom it seems to have been transmitted as the standard exegesis of the *Parmenides*.[9] Plotinus's mysticism gave the doctrine more life and meaning than it had ever had, and his vastly superior intelligence enabled him to come nearer than any of his predecessors to fusing it into a harmonious whole with the Aristotelian and Stoic parts of his philosophical inheritance; though even he did not completely succeed.

The discovery of the negative conception of the One, as unpredicable and absolute Unity, in the tradition before Plotinus, makes considerably less likely the theory of Heinemann[10] of the early

[1] "The *Parmenides* of Plato and the Neo-Platonic One", *C.Q.* vol. XXII, 1928, p. 136.

[2] *Met.* A, 6. 987b. 25.

[3] *In Met.* 925b. 27 ff.

[4] Dodds, *l.c.*

[5] See above, Ch. 1; Dodds, p. 132, n. 3.

[6] Witt, *Albinus*, p. 19; Dodds, *l.c.*

[7] Above, Ch. 1.

[8] Above, Ch. 1.

[9] *Enn.* V. 1. 3. Taylor, *Parmenides*, App. E, pp. 147–8.

[10] Pp. 120 ff.

development of Plotinus's thought. Heinemann postulates a "Platonic" period, represented by the five treatises of Porphyry's first group which, on internal evidence, he regards as Plotinus's earliest works.[1] In this period, he alleges, the supreme principle of the system was the Platonic transcendent Good, not yet the characteristically Neo-Platonic One; further, he finds that even the full Plotinian conception of Νοῦς is absent. He holds that in the "second section of the first period" of Plotinus's thought, the conceptions of Νοῦς and the One were evolved from the original scheme (material world—Soul—Good) by a process of abstraction[2]—a sort of "layering" or perpetual mental division of entities into form and matter, of which it is certainly possible to find instances in Plotinus, notably in his treatment of the connection between Soul and the material world.

It must be conceded that Heinemann is right in denying that the conception of the One as Unity-Absolute appears in these treatises. The only exception is in the last words of IV. 2. 2, which fit rather awkwardly on to what precedes and read very like a gloss. They may well be a comment or summing-up by Porphyry.[3] Elsewhere in these treatises the supreme principle, though, like the Platonic Good, it transcends being,[4] is not ever actually spoken of as the One, or in terms of the "negative theology". For Νοῦς the evidence is much less conclusive. Heinemann's case[5] depends on the rejection, at least from this treatise, of the chapters of IV. 7 printed in the Budé edition as 8. 1–5, the text of which occurs only in Eusebius[6] and in a Renaissance MS[7] which probably takes it from Eusebius, as both Kirchhoff and Volkmann[8] think. In Ch. 8 (3), (11) Νοῦς is clearly mentioned in the normal Plotinian relation to Soul and to the supreme principle or god. There seems, however, no real reason for rejecting these chapters. They fit perfectly with their context and carry on the thread of the argument, and agree with the rest of the treatise in

[1] IV. 7; IV. 2; I. 2; I. 6; I. 3.
[2] Pp. 138 ff.
[3] Heinemann, p. 101; cp. p. 123.
[4] I. 3. 5.
[5] Pp. 128–9.
[6] *Praep. Ev.* XV. 22; XV. 10.
[7] Marcianus A, 240.
[8] Vol. II, Introd. pp. 26–7 of his edition.

their mingled dependence on and criticism of the Peripatetic doctrines of the soul.[1]

The main objections to Heinemann's belief in this early, Oneless period of Plotinus's thought are, first that his chronological re-ordering of the treatises rests on very shaky foundations. His main argument is drawn from somewhat rash assertions about references in one treatise to another[2] by which he tries to discredit Porphyry's arrangement of the individual treatises within the main groups. A more serious objection is the presence of a doctrine of the transcendent One in the tradition before Plotinus. It is difficult, in any case, to assume any very marked change or development in Plotinus's thought when we remember that his writings were all concentrated into a comparatively short period at the end of his life; he began to write at the age of forty-nine, and his whole output is contained within the space of fifteen years. It is, however, just possible to follow Heinemann in postulating a period after Plotinus began to write when he had not yet come to regard his supreme principle as the Neo-Pythagorean Unity-Absolute. It is more difficult to assume that he did not know of systems at the head of which this Unity-Absolute stood. Neo-Pythagorean authors were read in his school.[3] Moderatus himself was known in the school of his contemporary the Christian Origen,[4] and may well have been known to Plotinus himself, as he was to Porphyry;[5] the interpretation of the *Parmenides* in terms of the theory was known to him as a normal and traditional exegesis.[6] It is almost certain that Plotinus must have known the doctrine from an early period of his life of study.

Heinemann's theory of the development of the One and Νοῦς by a process of abstraction must be uncompromisingly rejected. We

[1] See Bréhier's introduction to this treatise in the Budé edition, and P. Henry, *Recherches sur le P.E. d'Eusèbe et l'édition perdue des œuvres de Plotin*, pp. 117–29.

[2] On this see Bréhier's introduction to his edition, pp. 18–20.

[3] Porph. *V.P.* Chs. 14, 15.

[4] Porph. ap. Euseb. *H.E.* VI. 19. 8; Dodds, p. 139.

[5] Simplicius, *in Phys.* A, 7. 230. 34 ff., Diels; Dodds, p. 136.

[6] Taylor, *Parmenides*, App. E, p. 147.

have seen that the elements of the full Plotinian account of both are to be found in the tradition. We have seen that Νοῦς was never at any stage an "abstraction" from the World-Soul but a supreme principle in its own right, deriving from the very positive Aristotelian conception of God, brought, before Plotinus rather clumsily, into some connection with the Platonic World of Ideas. The "abstractness" of the One was also a feature in the tradition. It arose partly from the desire to stress its transcendence, partly, perhaps, from a confusion due to the incursion of Speusippus's "potential" One into the tradition and the consequent developments of Neo-Pythagoreanism and interpretation of the *Parmenides*. Heinemann substitutes a process of abstraction, of the splitting-up of concepts, in the mind of Plotinus (for which there is no real evidence) for the real, historical development of ideas.

We must not, of course, make the mistake of trying to explain Plotinus's system entirely from its historical antecedents. Plotinus was an original genius of the first rank; and we must search, so far as we can without falling into subjectivism and unbridled imagination, into his personal thought and spiritual life for the reasons which led him to adopt and adapt the elements in the tradition in the way he did. In particular, we must try to see clearly why he retained such incompatible views of his First Principle and made such heroic attempts to reconcile them. We can account for it partly, but not wholly, as a surrender to the complexity of his tradition.

We must first of all remember, that, though I have separated the "positive" and "negative" conceptions of the One very sharply for the purpose of enquiring into their historical origins, they are not in fact so separated. There are many connecting links and half-way stages between them. The most important of these is the very Platonic conception of the One as the principle of Measure,[1] cause of the imposition of limit and order on the indefinite, and so of reality.[2] Plotinus insists always that the unit or standard of measure, the formal principle that produces good or truth is always other

[1] v. 5. 4.

[2] See Bréhier, pp. 137 ff., 164–5. For Measure in Plato see *Politicus*, 283 d, 284 e.

than, above and outside, that which it produces, measures, or limits. This principle is represented in its simplest and most general form by the phrase ἡ ποσότης αὐτὴ οὐ ποσόν.[1] It is applied to ethics[2] and, most frequently of all, to the formation of τὰ νοητά through the making definite of the indefinite movement of Νοῦς towards the One as principle of limit.[3] This conception of the One as giver of form is strongly "positive". It passes at once into the conception of the One as Father, Maker distinct from what he makes,[4] Giver of good, beauty, truth, in fact as God in a sense not very far removed from that of Christian theology. This positive conception is, however, expressed in negative terms, and given the Neo-Pythagorean conception of the Mathematical One as source of number, of the principle of measure, limit, form, in the universe, it can very easily slide over into the negative, of the One as an unpredicable unity, which lies behind the Neo-Pythagorean exegesis of the *Parmenides*. All that is necessary for this doubleness of idea, this confusion of thought, to get into the tradition, is that the source of number, of mathematical pattern and order, should be identified with the ground of being, the principle which causes things to be what they are. Speusippus, and perhaps the Pythagorean tradition represented by the fragments of Philolaus, did not make this mistake. The real ground of being for them was the totality of mathematical order, symbolized by or consisting of the Tetractys, not the original One. The Neo-Pythagoreans, however, introduced the confusion and Plotinus followed them.

It must be noted, of course, at this point, that Plotinus was fully conscious of the inadequacy of the term "One" to express all he meant to convey by his description of his First Principle. He denies passionately any intention to limit it, to make any positive statement about it by using this name. Such an attempt at a positive, clear statement about the One, he says, would only result in worse confusion.[5] Inge[6] suggests that Plotinus only uses the word "One" because the Greeks had no symbol for zero. What he calls One

[1] II. 4. 9.
[2] I. 2. 2.
[3] V. 1. 5, 3. 10; VI. 7. 15–21.
[4] III. 9. 3.
[5] V. 5. 6.
[6] *The Philosophy of Plotinus*, II, pp. 107–8.

Scotus Erigena, and also some of the mystics of the Christian tradition, call Nothing. It must, however, I think, be admitted that in using the term Plotinus brought with it a great deal of the content it had acquired in the philosophical tradition which preceded him.[1] In trying to give some account of his ineffable First Principle he uses the conception which he found already existing in this tradition. This is a fact to which M. Bréhier, in his otherwise admirable discussion of the doctrine of the One, does not allow sufficient importance. Even in the passage already quoted,[2] where Plotinus is doing his very best to avoid making his terms too definite and dragging down the Supreme into the region of speech and logical thinking, he says that "the name One perhaps conveys a negation of multiplicity" (ἄρσιν ἔχει πρὸς τὰ πολλά). This, together with his reference in the next sentence to the Pythagorean identification of the One with Apollo and the appalling "mystical" pun which accompanies it (ἀποφάσει τῶν πολλῶν), definitely puts the One in a Neo-Pythagorean context. In Plotinus's descriptions of the One we have, as elsewhere in the *Enneads*, a profound and sensitive, if at times somewhat confused, account of the spiritual life poured into the mould of an already complex metaphysical tradition.

[1] Cp. Arnou, *Désir de Dieu*, pp. 62–3. [2] v. 5. 6.

Chapter III

THE ONE AND THE SPIRITUAL LIFE

To arrive at a deeper perception of the reasons for Plotinus's development or retention of such conflicting conceptions of the One we must turn from considering his system as a metaphysical structure and study it as an account of the spiritual life. It is in this aspect that his system possesses the greatest vitality and originality. One of the main objects of such a study must be to determine what exactly we mean when we use the term "negative theology" in discussing Plotinus's philosophy. On the surface, the meaning of the term appears to be straightforward enough. It expresses an assertion of the transcendence of the Supreme Principle by denying that its nature can be adequately expressed by any term or definition. It will be found nevertheless, on closer examination, that there are several roads of negation and that they lead to very different conceptions of the Supreme. In Plotinus's thought it seems possible to distinguish three forms of "negative theology", which may be called, for lack of less clumsy descriptions: (i) the Mathematical Negative Theology, or Negative Theology of the Tradition; (ii) the Negative Theology of Positive Transcendence; (iii) the Negative Theology of the Infinite Subject.

The first has already been sufficiently dealt with. To sum up, it regards the First Principle as the principle of measure or limit which transcends what it measures or limits, and also as an unpredicable unity standing at the origin of number. It is primarily a mathematical-metaphysical and epistemological conception, and carries with it little depth of religious feeling. Indeed we have found it in Speusippus explicitly detached from all religious or ethical considerations. Its importance in Plotinus's religious thought is as part of its metaphysical framework and background.[1]

[1] One form of this negative theology found in the Middle Platonists and perhaps borrowed by them from the Neo-Pythagoreans is the

The "theology of positive transcendence" is the religious aspect of the "positive" conception of the One treated in my first chapter.[1] What I wish to make clearer about it here is the attitude of the soul to the Supreme which it implies, the sense in which the One is presented here as the God of religion. Plotinus's metaphysics and his theology (using the words in a loose modern sense) are only two aspects of the same thing, and his piety is certainly a pietas philosophica. All the same, it is possible, as I have done in my first chapter, to emphasize one side at the expense of the other. I now wish to redress the balance.

If the One is regarded as the First Cause, making and preserving all below it,[2] and consequently its transcendence, its "otherness" and superiority to that which it makes are stressed,[3] the corresponding spiritual attitude to it is one of religious worship. It may be spoken of as "beyond being" and all the terms of the "negative theology" at its most emphatic may be applied to it; but it will be clear that this is only because its reality cannot be adequately expressed in terms of the realities we know; phrases are preferred which make it clear that the transcendent reality is more than what is denied of it. It is "light above light".[4] VI. 8 is the classic treatise for this theology of transcendence. It may be well summed up in the words of the great English Benedictine mystic, Father Augustine Baker: "And when she [the soul] being in such case of nothing, apprehending God as nothing—that is as no imaginable or intelligible thing, but as another thing which is above all images and species, and is expressible by no species...doth further apply and add her aforesaid nothing to the nothing of God, then remaineth there, neither in respect of the soul nor in respect of God, anything but a certain vacuity or nothing. In which nothing is acted and passeth a union between God and the soul....And so in this case of union there is nothing and nothing, and they make nothing....This is the state of perfect union, which is termed by some a state of nothing, and

analogy from geometrical abstraction (plane from line, line from point, etc.). See Witt, *Albinus*, p. 132; Dodds, *Proclus*, pp. 31–2.

[1] For the religious side of the conception, see especially pp. 2–6.

[2] VI. 7. 23.

[3] III. 8. 9, 9. 3; V. 3. 12; VI. 7. 21–2.

[4] V. 3. 12, 15.

by others with as much reason a state of totality; because there God is seen and enjoyed in it, and He therein as the container of all things[1] and the soul as it were lost in Him."[2]

It is clear that in this passage the "nothingness" of both the soul and God implies no mathematical or metaphysical assertions. The soul is "nothing" simply in virtue of her utter forgetfulness of all the world and its business, and especially of herself. God is seen by the soul as "nothing" in that He transcends everything that she can say about Him. He is not thought of as an unpredicable unity or as non-existent even in the sense of "transcending being"; He is "another thing which is above all images and species".

The essential element in worship is the otherness of the object of worship from the worshipper. When the One is thought of as God, as the transcendent, worshipful "being above being", it is impossible for the mystical union to be thought of, as it is so often in Plotinus, as the realization of a pre-existing identity; that is, it is impossible for it to be so thought of when the attention is concentrated on the fact of the religious experience. When it comes to detailed exposition of his theological position Plotinus remains constant to his view of the continuity of divine and human.[3] The doctrine of the continuity of the One and the human soul does not, of course, exclude the possibility of a real "otherness", a vividly felt difference-in-unity, between them. Indeed, the two things are closely connected in Plotinus's most characteristic thought.[4] It is because "all things are in the One",[5] organically connected to the One,[6] that the mystical union can be for the philosopher the culmination of a purely natural process, needing no grace, no raising or transforming of his nature into a supernatural way of life. There is, however, a real difference of emphasis, according to whether the main stress is laid on the underlying, pre-existing unity and on the

[1] Cp. *Enn.* V. I. 8, 9, 10.

[2] Fr. Augustine Baker, *Remains*, quoted in Dom Justin McCann's edition of *The Cloud of Unknowing*, p. 401. There is a very good summing up of this kind of "negative theology" by Plotinus himself in V. 5. 13 and VI. 7. 38. Cp. also Proclus, *in Parm.* VI. 43–9.

[3] V. 2. I, 2.

[4] Cp. Bréhier, pp. 157–69.

[5] V. 5. 9.

[6] V. 3. 12; V. 2. I, 2.

unifying element in the experience[1] or on the "shock", the "sentiment d'une présence" (Bréhier),[2] the intense perception at once of the Supreme as wholly other and yet of being united with that other, which is also a most vital element in the experience.[3] This latter is the culmination of that attitude of exaltation of the Supreme and that note, one might say, of religious devotion towards It, which is especially prominent in the treatises VI. 7–9.

It is this tone of passionate devotion towards the Supreme, this exaltation and praise of It, which is perhaps the most clearly un-Hellenic thing in Plotinus. He may himself derive it from the teaching of the *Symposium*,[4] but it goes far beyond anything in Plato, far beyond the ordered ascent under the driving impulse of Eros from physical beauty, through the beauty of laws and institutions and of the sciences, to the purely intellectual contemplation of the Idea.[5] Plato could never have said that the beauty of the realm of Νοῦς, that is the beauty of τὰ νοητά, of the Ideas, was "ἀργός till it receives a light from the good", that the Intellectual Beauty needed a χάρις ἐπιθέουσα τῷ κάλλει from That which is above it to move the beholder;[6] nor could he have described the Idea of the Good in Plotinus's impassioned, awe-inspiring language with its imagery from Hellenistic mysteries.[7] The Greek, and Plato remains on this point, I think, thoroughly Greek, was not given to passionate devotion to his gods. He may (as in Orphism) have a passionate desire to rise to their level, to be united with them in order to become divine, but he does not desire or worship God for God's sake. Plotinus at any rate comes very near to doing so.

We need not, however, seek for any very exotic origin for this un-Hellenic spirit of devotion in Plotinus. It was well established in

[1] V. 8. 11; VI. 9. 10; VI. 5. 12. [2] P. 157; VI. 7. 31.

[3] Cp. VI. 7. 34, where, though Soul and One are said to be ἓν ἄμφω, there is yet a most vivid realization throughout that they are two, not one; a pair of lovers united in their ecstasy, not a single principle in its primal absence of differentiation, as in VI. 5. 12.

[4] Cp. his commentary in III. 5. 5–10.

[5] *Symposium*, 210 A ff.

[6] VI. 7. 22; a chapter which is most illuminating on the difference between the goal of Eros in Plato and in Plotinus. Cp. Bréhier, p. 146.

[7] VI. 9. 11.

the tradition of Greek thought centuries before his time. It entered the Greek world, it seems, with the Stoics. The note is already sounded in the Hymn of Cleanthes[1] and recurs again and again in later Stoicism.[2] It is true that there are important differences; not only is Plotinus's philosophical view of the nature of the Supreme very different from that of the Stoics and theoretically, at any rate in the aspect which we are now considering, better adapted to this sort of devotional feeling; but, what is more important for our present purpose, the Stoic devotion is bound up with a belief in the Divine Providence, a concentration on God's ordering of the world and its benefits to man,[3] which is absent in Plotinus, and is, indeed, incompatible with his view of πρόνοια and of the divine action in the world.[4] It may, perhaps, be said that while the objectivity of Plotinus's devotion to the Supreme is Platonist-Aristotelian, its passion is Stoic,[5] or at least is the result of that stream of intense religious feeling from the East which makes its first entry into the Graeco-Roman world with Stoicism. The union of the two, the exaltation of the remoteness and transcendence of the Supreme with the passionate devotion to the ruling principle of the universe, seems to be an original achievement of Plotinus. His Middle Platonist and Neo-Pythagorean predecessors, Albinus and Numenius, show little trace of religious feeling; nor is the spirit of devotion prominent in the *Hermetica*. We cannot, however, overlook the possibility of some influence of that "solar theology" so popular in Plotinus's time of which a rather distinctive form appears in the *Hermetica*,[6] and which seems to have had a profound influence on Plotinus's theory of the relation of the One to the rest of reality,[7] in spite of his far-reaching criticism of it in the Sixth Ennead.[8]

1 *St. Vet. Fragm.* I. 537.

2 Epictet. *Diss.* I. 6. 23, 16. 16; II. 10. 1; IV. 10. 14, etc.

3 Bidez, *Cité du Monde et Cité du Soleil*, pp. 253–4; Epictet. *l.c.*

4 III. 2. 1, 8. 3–4; IV. 4. 26, 42.

5 Cp. Bidez, *l.c.* for the contrast between the two attitudes.

6 XVI. 6 (Scott).

7 Cp. my article "Emanation in Plotinus", *Mind*, Jan. 1937 and below, Ch. IV.

8 VI. 4, 5. Cp. Bréhier, pp. 116–17.

We may agree with Dodds[1] that the evidence for any influence on Plotinus of contemporary Oriental mystery-religions (as distinct from "solar theology") is so slight as to prove nothing, and that the assumption of such an influence misrepresents the character of Plotinus's thought.

We may note that it is from this aspect of Plotinus's thought that his influence on orthodox Christian thinking derives. It must always seem strange to those who regard Plotinus primarily as a monistic idealist that his influence, through St Augustine,[2] on Western Catholic philosophical and theological thought should have been so considerable. It would be natural enough that he should influence the Arab philosophers of the Middle Ages whose thought was far removed from the central traditions of Islam, Christianity, or Judaism, or isolated and unorthodox individuals like Scotus Erigena, or Schelling and the German idealists. When, however, it comes to discovering parallels between the thought of Plotinus and that of St Thomas Aquinas, as Dean Inge, for instance, quite legitimately does,[3] we must begin to feel that the idealist element in him has been over-stressed, and that more attention must be paid to that aspect of his thought which I have just been considering. It would, all the same, be a mistake to go too far in the opposite direction. The vast extent of Plotinus's influence on subsequent thought is due very largely to his inconsistency.

We must now turn to what I have called the Negative Theology of the Infinite Subject, or Infinite Self. In this the negation consists in the denial of all limitation, of all definite frontier between subject and object, the Self and the All, and sometimes the One. In it, ultimately, object is swallowed up by subject and, as the mind realizes its identity with the higher realms of being, all things are resolved into a unity in which knowledge and consciousness, in the

[1] "The *Parmenides* of Plato and the Neo-Platonic One", *C.Q.* vol. XXII, 1928, pp. 129–30, 141.

[2] On Plotinus and St Augustine, too important a subject to be discussed parenthetically here, see P. Henry, S. J., "Augustine and Plotinus", *Journal of Theological Studies*, vol. XXXVII, Jan. 1937, No. 149 and *Plotin et l'Occident* (Louvain, 1934).

[3] Inge, *Philosophy of Plotinus*, vol. I, p. 15.

ordinary sense of the word, become impossible.[1] This indefinite expansion of the self, this denial of all limitation, generally stops for Plotinus at the realm of Νοῦς, the All or One-Being, and it is at this point that we find it most strikingly expressed, especially in the two treatises of the Sixth Ennead in which Plotinus criticizes the contemporary "solar theology".[2] It is at times, however, carried as far as the One. Even the last barrier is broken down, and man finds his supreme self-realization in identity with the supreme principle.[3] The One is the primary or absolute self, πρώτως αὐτὸς καὶ ὑπερόντως αὐτός.[4] For this reason, and because it is a real form of the "negative theology" in that it annuls description and definition along with separation and consciousness, it will be as well to discuss it here. Bréhier and Heinemann have described this aspect of Plotinus's thought so well that I do not wish to enlarge on it; though I think they have given it too much importance in their general estimate of his system. What I wish to do is to draw attention to some points concerning its origin and its limitations. M. Bréhier has put forward a very attractive theory of the origin of this way of thinking in Plotinus, which he traces to Indian sources.[5] This theory I have in the past attempted to criticize.[6] There does, however, seem to remain, when every attempt has been made to find approximations to this doctrine, or ways of thought leading to it, in the Hellenic tradition, a certain residuum, or rather a sort of general character pervading much of the *Enneads*, which it is not easy to account for on a purely Hellenic basis. The un-Hellenic element which may possibly be present in Plotinus's thought is not something that can be discovered by analysis, but rather by contemplation of the whole from certain aspects. This task M. Bréhier has performed very adequately. It will, however, be worth while to examine shortly any approximations or preparations for Plotinus's doctrine which may be discoverable in previous Greek thought, as they will

[1] Cp. Heinemann, pp. 299 ff., "Die Erkenntnislehre" and Bréhier, pp. 69–71, 122–33, 181–6.

[2] See especially VI. 4. 7 and VI. 5. 1, 12; cp. V. 8. 7, 11.

[3] VI. 9. 7, 11; VI. 7. 36.

[4] VI. 8. 14; cp. V. 1. 11.

[5] Bréhier, pp. 107–33 (L'Orientalisme de Plotin).

[6] "Plotinus and India", *C.Q.* vol. XXX, 1936, pp. 22–9.

help towards an understanding of the limitations of the Plotinian theory which is important for our present purposes.

It does not seem easy to find much trace of this side of Plotinus's doctrine in his immediate predecessors. It is entirely absent from Middle Platonism and Neo-Pythagoreanism. The case of the Stoics is more debatable; but even they do not seem to have reached the doctrine of the "infinite self". The "pantheism" or "monism" of the earlier Stoics can easily be exaggerated. There seems to be a real dualism between ποιοῦν and πάσχον, θεός or λόγος and ὕλη;[1] and still more important, in spite of the assertion of the organic unity of the universe,[2] the Stoics tended in practice to think of it as a community or society of distinct individuals. The doctrine of the ἰδίως ποιόν[3] is incompatible with genuine pantheism, with a real recognition of the identity of part and whole, individual and All. This individualism extends to the Stoic epistemology. Truths are thought of as existing in isolation. The relation between τὸ ἀληθές and ἡ ἀλήθεια is compared to that between the citizen and the δῆμος, and the δῆμος is described as τὸ ἐκ πολλῶν πολιτῶν ἄθροισμα, a collection of individuals held together in a more or less organic corporate unity by a single law, but still remaining individuals.

Here we see what is perhaps the most essential and characteristic element in early Stoic thought, the conception of the City of the Cosmos, the universality of which both men and gods are citizens and of which the star-gods are the rulers.[4] God is often thought of as the Universal Law, by which men, as inhabitants of the Universal City, are bound together.[5] It is true that the unity of this cosmic city is in a very real sense an organic unity. God is not only the Universal Law but the One Life permeating all things, vitalizing and unifying them.[6] There seems always, however, to have been a

[1] Cp. S.V.F. II. 301–3, etc., 527; Bréhier, *Chrysippe*, pp. 148–9: the two are indeed closely united. The active cause is ἀχώριστος τῆς ὕλης, συμμεμιγμένη, S.V.F. II. 306–8, 310, but it is a union of two things, a unity in duality.

[2] ζῷον...λογικὸν καὶ ἔμψυχον καὶ νοερόν, S.V.F. II. 633.

[3] S.V.F. II. 395–7. Cp. Bréhier, *Chrysippe*, p. 154.

[4] Cp. Bidez, *Cité du Monde et Cité du Soleil*, esp. pp. 256–62.

[5] Bréhier, *Chrysippe*, pp. 212–13.

[6] E.g. S.V.F. II. 1021.

certain dualism, as I said above, between the One Life and that which it vivifies, most strikingly expressed in Zeno's metaphor of the honey in the honeycomb.[1] Further, the individual parts always remain separate and distinct, from each other and from the whole; there is no interpenetration of whole and parts. The nearest approach in early Stoic doctrine, not to the theory of the "infinite self" but to a crude and materialistic foreshadowing of it, is to be found in the doctrine of κρᾶσις δι' ὅλων, of the total interpenetration of bodies.[2] It is tempting to think that this doctrine may have had some effect in stimulating thinkers dissatisfied with Stoic materialism to work out more clearly the implications of immateriality, and the possibilities revealed by an understanding of the conception of spiritual reality unconfined by the limitations of space and time. It is possible that there may be a connection between this aspect of Stoic thought and Plotinus's doctrine of omnipresence. It is not, however, I think, possible to show that there is any direct influence of the one on the other. In II. 7. 2 and 3 Plotinus simply accepts the κρᾶσις δι' ὅλων theory, in so far as he does accept it, from the point of view of his own theory of ὕλη. In fact, it is difficult to see what connection there could be, other than the rather negative and indirect one which I have already suggested, between this rather crude piece of Stoic physics and the subtle doctrine, depending upon a profound understanding of the nature of immateriality, of the "infinite self", the identity of whole and part.

In that later Stoicism which is generally supposed to derive from Posidonius I can find little more approach to the doctrine of the "infinite self". There is perhaps a movement towards a pantheism more genuine than is to be found in the earlier Stoics,[3] but there does not seem to be much evidence for the statement that in Posidonius

[1] S.V.F. I. 155, 156; cp. II. 1041, etc.

[2] Cp. Alex. Aphrod. *de Mixtione*, pp. 216, 14, 226, 34; S.V.F. II. 473, 475; also *Enn.* II. 7, where in Ch. 2 Plotinus gives a distinctive form of his own to the doctrine.

[3] Cp. Bréhier, *Chrysippe*, p. 149; though the passage he quotes from Seneca (*Ep.* 92, 30): "Totum hoc quo continemur et unum est et deus; et socii sumus eius et membra", suggests the persistence of the old idea of the cosmos as an ἄθροισμα of individuals.

"Subjekt und Objekt...sich einen und durchdringen".[1] It is true, probably, that the belief that the universe is an organism goes back to Posidonius, and possibly that Plotinus transferred this organic character from the visible to the intelligible world, a transference on which I shall have occasion to comment more fully later. It is also true that the Neo-Platonic stress on unity as the essential principle of being, and the account of the stages of unification, go back most likely also to Posidonius.[2] There is, however, no evidence that this conception of organic unity was accompanied by that application of Aristotelian psychology which resulted in the doctrine of "spiritual interpenetration", which is fundamental to the conception of the "infinite self". The later Stoics might think of the self as an organic part of the All; but they did not identify the two. They did not say "The part *is* the whole". Their doctrines did not lead them to that final paradox of Plotinian "pantheism"—καίτοι καὶ πρότερον ἦσθα πᾶς ἀλλ' ὅτι καὶ ἄλλο τι προσῆν σοι μετὰ τὸ πᾶν, ἐλάττων ἐγίνου τῇ προσθήκῃ.[3]

There is, however, one point at which this later Stoicism comes very close to Plotinus's doctrine. This is in such passages as Marcus Aurelius's description of the boundlessness of the soul, εἰς τὴν ἀπειρίαν τοῦ αἰῶνος ἐκτείνεται.[4] Here, with the assertion that the human mind has the power of containing, by comprehending, the All, we are well on our way towards the denial of any boundary between the All and the self. This looks strikingly like a reminiscence of Heracleitus's ψυχῆς πείρατα οὐκ ἂν ἐξεύροιο πᾶσαν ἐπιπορευόμενος ὁδόν· οὕτω βαθὺν λόγον ἔχει.[5] We are not, however, I think, dealing here simply with a Stoic exegesis of Heracleitus, still less with a genuine return to a "Heracleitean" way of thought, however

[1] Reinhardt, *Kosmos und Sympathie*, p. 120. On the question of Posidonius's mysticism cp. J. F. Dobson, "The Posidonius Myth", *C.Q.* vol. XII, 1918, p. 179.

[2] Cf. W. Theiler, *Vorbereitung des Neu-Platonismus*, pp. 61–end; Witt, "Plotinus and Posidonius", *C.Q.* vol. XXIV, 1930, p. 198. The One of Plotinus may perhaps be regarded from one aspect as a hypostatization of the immanent principle of unity which for the later Stoics was the source of reality, see especially VI. 4.

[3] *Enn.* VI. 5. 12.

[4] XI. 1. Cp. Sen. *Ep.* 92, 30.

[5] Fr. 71, Bywater.

tempting it may be to try to connect the doctrine of the "infinite self" with certain aspects of Heracleitus's thought as represented in his fragments.[1] What we seem to be dealing with, in passages like that quoted from Marcus Aurelius, is a continuation and development, doubtless under the influence of the "Posidonian" conviction of the organic unity of the universe, of that tradition of Greek epistemology which finds its culmination in Aristotle. It is, surprisingly, to Aristotle, the champion, it would seem, of objective rationalism, that we must turn to find the nearest approach that can be found in the purely Hellenic philosophical tradition to a source for Plotinus's doctrine of the "infinite self".

The two Aristotelian doctrines which seem to serve as ground or foundation for the "infinite self" in Plotinus are, that the mind becomes what it thinks,[2] and that there exists an "active reason" which is impersonal and universal.[3] According to the first passage referred to, the intellect apart from its object is a pure potentiality. It can only have actual existence in so far as it receives and is informed by the object known. This is an extension to the intellect of a principle already established for sense-perception,[4] and in that connection put forward as solving the traditional dispute between the theories of "knowledge of like by like" and "knowledge of unlike by unlike". It is worth noting that both sides of this Pre-Socratic controversy assert the continuity of subject and object, and that knowledge is for them only possible because of this continuity, because knower and known are of the same stuff, or because man and the external world both contain the same "pairs of opposites". It is on the recognition of this feature of Greek epistemology, developed by Aristotle with greater subtlety to fit in with his genuinely immaterial conception of the soul, that the case for some sort of a Hellenic pedigree for Plotinus's theory of the "infinite self" really rests. There are, roughly speaking, four stages. First,

[1] E.g. his attacks on πολυμαθίη (frs. 16, 17), the objective, rational knowledge of the Pythagoreans, his repeated allusions to the λόγος common to all men, his phrase ἐδιζησάμην ἐμεωυτόν (fr. 80).

[2] *De An.* III. 4. 429a; cp. *Met.* Λ, 7. 1072b.

[3] *De An.* III. 5. 430a.

[4] II. 5. 418a.

the recognition that knowledge is due to a certain community of nature between the knowing subject and the known object. Second, the development from this of the Aristotelian doctrine that the mind "becomes what it thinks". Then we have the recognition of the fact that, as a result of this conception of knowledge, the human mind can in a sense contain by comprehending the All, that its frontiers are as wide as those of reality; in Plotinus's formulation, that the part can include the whole, that the whole and every part can be in every other part.[1] Then, the last development, the assertion that in its innermost reality the human mind is identical with the Absolute Self, the boundless totality of being, and even the transcendent supreme principle. There is, however, a considerable gulf between these last conceptions, between that of a spiritual interpenetrating unity-in-multiplicity and that of the single, boundless infinity, both self and principle of all reality, which absorbs all being and annihilates all distinction. It is just at this point that Bréhier, not without much plausibility, postulates an irruption of Indian thought into Plotinus's system. It is therefore interesting to discover, in our second Aristotelian doctrine, some evidence that the conception would not have seemed altogether strange to a Greek mind. The doctrine in question is that of the Νοῦς χωριστός, the "active reason" of the *De Anima*.[2] Whatever view we take of this rather mysterious passage it certainly involves the conception of the highest and most important part of the soul as a separable impersonal entity, the same for all men, persisting unchanged above the ebb and flow of individual existence. This clearly at once breaks down the conception of a finite, limited self or ego, clearly marked off from the rest of reality. It is clear, too, that the moments when the passive or potential reason is most perfectly assimilated to the active reason are the moments at which man's intellectual life reaches its highest level. It seems probable that, in Aristotle's thought, at those times of which he speaks when we live a life of contemplation like that of

[1] v. 8. 9; cp. vi. 7. 12–15, especially Ch. 14. The separateness and limitation of parts is for Plotinus a characteristic of the material universe, not to be transferred to the intelligible, as these passages show. Interpenetrability is an essential characteristic of the beings of the noetic world.

[2] iii. 5. 430a.

God,[1] "the partition between active and passive reason is broken down and we become aware of our oneness with the principle whose knowledge is always actual and complete".[2]

Here again we have a striking likeness to Plotinus. For him, too, the realization of our oneness with the Supreme is the crown and culmination of our supernatural life, and something that comes but rarely. It is true that we must not press the comparison too far. The mystical union in Plotinus is something very different from the Theoria of Aristotle, and so is his account of the abiding of the soul in Νοῦς. Between the two lies the irruption of Stoicism into the world of Greek thought, changing its whole tone and temper. Plotinus's thought and language are coloured all through by this element in the tradition he inherited, by the Stoic insistence on the oneness of all things and the passionate Stoic devotion to the all-pervading Divine Life. It must be remembered, too, that it is unlikely that Aristotle identified the Active Reason with his god.[3] Alexander of Aphrodisias, however, did do so,[4] and not only do we know from Porphyry[5] that Alexander was read in Plotinus's school but there are several passages in the *Enneads*[6] in which Plotinus either directly or by unmistakable allusion identifies his Νοῦς, which for him is equivalent to Aristotle's God, with the Active or Separable Reason. The extension of this identification of Self and All to the identification of Self and One arises partly from the nature of the mystical experience itself and partly from the tendency inherent in this way of thought for all frontiers, even the last, to disappear, and for Νοῦς to pass imperceptibly into the One.[7] The realization of identity with the One, however, is for Plotinus nearly always temporary; and the fact that the process of self-realization, as such, normally stops at the realizing of the identity of self and Νοῦς-All confirms the view of the transcendent relation of the One to Νοῦς put forward in my first chapter.

1 *Met.* Λ, 7. 1072b. 14, 24; *Eth. N.* 1177b. 26–1178a. 8; 1178b. 18–32.
2 Ross, *Aristotle*, p. 150.
3 Ross, pp. 152–3; Hicks, *De An.* Introd. pp. lxiv–lxix.
4 Alex. *De An.* 80. 16–92. 11; Mantissa, 106. 19–113. 24.
5 *Life*, Ch. 14.
6 v. 11–12 (cp. I. 4. 9; v. 8. 11); v. 9. 3–4.
7 Cp. VI. 9. 9 and my discussion in Ch. IV of VI. 4, 5.

We have found, then, a firm foundation for Plotinus's theory of the "infinite self" in Aristotle's psychology; given the two doctrines that the mind becomes what it thinks, and can therefore, as Marcus Aurelius saw, stretch itself boundlessly over the All, and that the highest part of the mind is separable, impersonal, eternal, universal, it is not a very long step to the doctrine as it appears in Plotinus. It is of particular interest here to note that the limitations of the Active Reason and of the Self identical with the All are to a great extent the same. No one, I suppose, would want to call Aristotle a pantheist. It would be nearly as misleading to apply the same title to Plotinus without very far-reaching limitations, and a limited pantheism is surely a contradiction in terms.[1] This is a conclusion of peculiar importance for the purposes of this study. If Plotinus were demonstrated to be a genuine pantheist, if the One-Self swallowed up the whole of reality, it would be impossible to consider Plotinus as the author of a system of metaphysics, in the sense of the constructor of an ordered, articulated picture of the complex structure of reality, of which we could consider the architecture and, so to speak, test the joints; just as, if the "mathematical-logical" conception of the One were proved to dominate Plotinus's thought, it would become impossible to bring the One into any sort of relation with reality. We must have a clear understanding of Plotinus's teaching on these points if we are to understand, not only what the philosophical system of Plotinus really is, but how there can be a philosophical system of Plotinus at all.

We find that in Plotinus, as in Alexander's interpretation of Aristotle, only the highest part of the human soul, among all the entities which we know, can be identified with the Divine or the One. Man must strip himself of all knowledge gained by sense-perception and discursive reason, of all the activities of the lower parts of the soul, must rise beyond Ψυχή and Νοῦς itself, before he can say that there is no more otherness left in him, that he has become the Seen, no longer the Seer.[2] This experience, too, like

[1] On the question of Plotinus's "pantheism" cp. Arnou, *Désir de Dieu*, pp. 182 ff., 283 ff.

[2] v. 8. 11; vi. 7. 35.

Aristotle's theoria, is temporary,[1] only to be enjoyed now and then for a short time. It is, however, the sharp differentiation between the human soul or self, with its power of realizing its unity with the Supreme, and the separation of the visible cosmos, which most clearly makes it impossible to call Plotinus a pantheist, or to exaggerate the importance of the doctrine of the Infinite Self. I shall deal more fully elsewhere with the relation of the material to the intelligible universe in Plotinus. Here it will be sufficient to point out the very marked separation of the material universe, of σῶμα, body or informed matter and its immanent directing principle, φύσις, from even the lowest of the great hypostases, from the transcendent ψυχή at whose level authentic intellectual and spiritual life, individual and universal, begins.[2] The whole argument on omnipresence in VI. 4 assumes and insists upon a real distinction between the Absolute and the relative.[3]

Our examination of Plotinus's system from the point of view of its "negative theology" does not seem, so far, to have brought us any nearer to a reconciliation or clarification of his complex and at times contradictory statements about the One. We have discovered from the point of view of metaphysics a tension between the conceptions of the One as Supreme Reality and the One as Mathematical Unity-Absolute, unpredicable and non-existent; and from the point of view of the spiritual life a tension between the conception of the One as God, transcendent, "wholly other", to be loved and worshipped, and the One as Absolute Self, identical with the human soul if it will but realize its own dignity. The only way, I think (apart from the examinations already carried out of the immensely complex traditional and inherited element in the *Enneads*), in which we can begin to understand the combination of these con-

[1] V. 5. 8, etc. [2] II. 3. 9; IV. 4. 18, 20, 27.

[3] Cp. especially Ch. 3. Even the phrase of 5. 12, "Thou wert All before, too; but something else other than the All was added to thee...", suggests a view closer to that of Parmenides as expounded by Cornford (*C.Q.* vol. XXVII, 1933, 2, p. 111) than to pantheism; a view, that is, of two worlds, side by side, the One-All, which alone is truly real, and the shifting contingent multiplicity of not fully real entities which cannot be the subject of true knowledge.

flicting ideas in Plotinus's theology is by a consideration of the mystical experience itself.

Before doing this, however, it will be advisable to give a little attention to the proportions in which these different elements are mingled in the *Enneads*. It can, I think, be said that the "positive" conception of the One is that which dominates; this is natural enough, for it is only on this conception that any philosophical system, or any extended and valid account of the religious life, can be based. The "positive" conception is implied in all those passages where the genuine theory of emanation, an efflux or radiation as of light, is spoken of,[1] and in all those in which the distinction between Νοῦς, universal or human, and the One, is spoken of as something permanent, not really transcended even in the mystical union.[2] The other views of the One, the "negative" and that which makes it the last stage in self-realization, occupy a relatively small place in the *Enneads*. It would be a grave mistake, however, to regard them as not really there, to try to explain them away as exaggerated expressions of the "positive" doctrine. It is necessary to realize their presence and their importance if we are to understand rightly the nature of Plotinus's thought, its pedigree and its later influence.

We are, however, I think, entitled to reject as exaggerated Heinemann's condemnation of Plotinus as a destroyer of all possibility of rational thinking, or Bréhier's evaluation of him as primarily a subjective idealist. Plotinus's normal, carefully qualified account of the supreme mystical union[3] does not give any justification for such a view.

There is no doubt that the core of Plotinus's philosophy, the source of the vitality of this thought, is to be found in his experience of the "mystical union". The passionately religious character of his writing about the Supreme, which springs from this, seems to run through all his works with the possible exception of those written before VI. 9. This treatise certainly seems to mark a deepening of the spiritual intensity of the *Enneads*. Porphyry speaks of Plotinus as

[1] I. 7. 1; V. 1. 2, 1. 7, 2. 1, 3. 10, 3. 12, 6. 4; VI. 8. 18, 9. 9, etc.

[2] III. 8. 11, 9. 3; V. 3. 11, etc.

[3] VI. 9. 10–11. Cp. Arnou, *Désir de Dieu*, pp. 246 ff.

having attained to the mystical union four times "while I was with him", a phrase which seems to suggest that he knew or believed that it had happened on some occasions before he became Plotinus's disciple. We must certainly fix the period of Plotinus's first attainment before his acquaintance with Porphyry, either at the time when he was writing the earliest treatises of the *Enneads* or still earlier. If we are to embark on the perilous task of trying to fix the date more exactly, it would seem best to put it just before the writing of VI. 9.

From the language in which Plotinus speaks of the "mystical union" it is clear that his experience was similar to that of the great mystics of other traditions. I must speak here with the utmost diffidence. I have no wish to be numbered with those persons full of nice religious sentiments who write pretty little handbooks on mysticism. In close dependence, however, on the great tradition of mystical writers it may be permissible to try to say something about the experience which will make the complexity, and at times the inconsistency, of Plotinus's account of it easier to understand.

The two features of the "mystical union" of particular importance for Plotinus's doctrine of the One are what may be called its simplicity and its transcendence. Simplicity is a characteristic both of the object apprehended and of the apprehension itself, in which there is no consciousness of any act or being distinct from the object. The experience is "simple" in the sense of single, completely unified. The object, too, is apprehended as "simple", as an absolute unity, of which any description (which must inevitably involve dissection or analysis) appears irrelevant and impertinent. It is easy to see how this simplicity of the experience could lead to the assertion of the doctrine of the Infinite or Absolute Self, the statement that Seer and Seen are one and the same, undivided and unbounded; and also how the simplicity of the object apprehended could lead even to the negative theology of flat denial, the acceptance of the traditional exegesis of the *Parmenides* which makes the One an unpredicable unity. It must be remembered that Plotinus, in his philosophical rationalization of an experience in itself beyond description, was not controlled by any strong and coherent religious tradition, but, as we have seen, by a rather incoherent philosophical one. It is not surprising then that we find differing accounts, and sometimes inconsistent ones, according to whichever aspect of the experience remained uppermost in Plotinus's mind.

The second character of the experience, transcendence, is very easy to confuse with simplicity. The two must, however, be distinguished if we are to form any clear idea of the relation of the experience of Plotinus to his system. Transcendence is not the completely single and simple character of the apprehended object in itself, but its complete otherness from and independence of all other objects. It indicates the way in which those other objects not only seem utterly unimportant but ultimately vanish from consciousness altogether. It thus carries with it an implied judgement of value, which is instantaneous, without deliberation, and impersonal. It involves the conviction that the object apprehended is so much more, so much beyond and above all other objects, as to differ from them not in degree but in kind, to *be* in quite another sense from that in which they are. This clearly leads to the "negative theology of positive transcendence", the "analogical" view of the One. For Plotinus the whole universe is an analogy of the One. It is not "this" and not "that", but "this" and "that" are images of it and derive from it. The mere mention of them gives a certain determination to our thought.

These two characteristics of the experience, simplicity and transcendence, are not in themselves necessarily contradictory. They only become so when the characteristic of simplicity is rationalized in the way already indicated. This rationalization is not really necessary to explain the mystical experience (so far as it can be explained). The unitive act leads by its very intensity to unconsciousness of everything outside itself and in fact, so far as consciousness implies distinction and differentiation, to unconsciousness of itself and its object. It does not therefore follow that the object as perceived by the intellect, which must necessarily make distinctions, does not really exist, that the intellectual perception is untrue. The way to the mystic union is for Plotinus through the knowledge of the One in multiplicity; the path to the One lies through the realm of Νοῦς. It seems to be true that in this world at least perfect love casts out clear knowledge. It does not, or should not, deny that it is a way to reality.

It will be more satisfactory to try to consider the permanent philosophical and religious value of Plotinus's doctrine of the One when we have a little more of his system under our eye, and in particular when we have seen the shifts to which he is put in trying to fit the Absolute into a Hellenic philosophical cosmos. Here I will only say that I prefer that conception of the One which we have seen to be most central in Plotinus's philosophy, that which I have called "positive". It seems preferable, on both philosophic and religious grounds, that our conception of the Supreme Principle should allow of the possibility of a philosophy which is more than a string of negations and a religion outside the mystical experience.

Section II. ΝΟΥΣ

Chapter IV

ΝΟΥΣ AS EMANATION

Plotinus's doctrine of Νοῦς is the fullest expression in his system of the universal later Hellenic belief in a totally unified cosmic order. It is also the means by which he tries to bring the absolute, transcendent One into the organic unity of such a cosmos. Νοῦς is the first stage in the emanation or procession of the universe from the One; and in Plotinus's account of it are to be found such attempts as he makes to supplement or improve upon the concept of emanation. The connection between the One and Νοῦς is the most vital point in the structure of Plotinus's system. We have already considered it from the point of view of the One. Now we must turn to consider it from the point of view of Νοῦς, and must also consider the relation of Νοῦς to what comes after it, Soul and the visible universe. In doing this we shall have to go into the question of what Plotinus really meant by "emanation" and what are the origins of the conception.

Νοῦς in Plotinus has clearly become something far more complex and important than the "second mind" or "second god" of the Middle Platonist tradition, of Numenius[1] and Albinus.[2] Its different aspects may be summarily classified as follows: (i) It is a radiation, or efflux from the One, like light from the sun. (ii) In a few passages it is conceived as the first unfolding of the potentialities of the One, which is a seed holding all things in potency. (iii) It is the highest phase of intellect, both human and universal, which, directly contemplating the One, apprehends it in multiplicity. (iv) With this last is closely connected the idea that Νοῦς proceeds from the One as a potency and is actualized by returning upon it in contemplation. (v) It is the Intellectual Cosmos, a world-organism which contains the archetypes of all things in the visible universe. As such it

[1] 25, 26, 30, Thedinga. [2] *Eisagoge*, Ch. 10.

possesses to the full that organic unity which the later, "Posidonian" Stoics had predicated of the visible, for them the only, cosmos, but which Plotinus had denied to it in any full or real sense. (vi) This aspect is to some extent connected with the psychological side of Νοῦς by considering it as a universe of interpenetrating spiritual beings each containing all the others organically united in its contemplation. These six aspects may be grouped under three general headings, Νοῦς as Emanation, Νοῦς as Mind, and Νοῦς as Universe.

I shall first of all examine the genuine conception of emanation which is bound up with the "positive" conception of the One and is expressed in metaphors of light. The conception expressed in the "seed" metaphor is a different one, bound up with a different view of the One, and requires separate treatment.

It may be as well before starting on this investigation to dispose of one question which is not likely to trouble anyone with any knowledge of Plotinus's thought, but which should be answered for the sake of completeness. This is, can any relationship be discovered between the "emanations" which are characteristic of the Gnostic systems of the second century and earlier and the conception of emanation in Plotinus? There are not many who are likely to maintain that any such connection exists. Mercifully that remarkably untruthful and misleading sort of generalization which lumped Neo-Platonists and Gnostics, Jews and Greeks together as representatives of a decadent, Orientalized sort of thought called "Alexandrian" has practically disappeared from the history of philosophy. The Gnostics and Plotinus move in different worlds of thought. Plotinus's doctrine of emanation is a serious attempt to solve the problem of how to bring the Supreme Principle into any relation with the organic universal whole. The Gnostic emanations are one of the few examples in European thought of that curious application of the imagination at its most unrestrained and irrational to philosophical and theological problems which is characteristic of the less intellectual sort of Indian thought and in particular of its decadent, Europeanized version, Theosophy. There are some traces of this sort of thing in later Neo-Platonism, with its indiscriminate acceptance of all the unnecessary entities of the "Chaldean" theology; though even here Hellenic rationalism asserts itself in an appalling ingenuity of systematization and classification. Nothing, however, of this fanciful irrationality is to be found in Plotinus. The Gnostic systems, if they can be called systems, seem to have been inspired partly by syncretism, by the desire to find a place in their spiritual world for every sort of being occurring in the religions or philosophies of which they had any knowledge;[1] and partly by the passion for the personification of abstract ideas characteristic of their age, to which the names of their aeons bear witness,[2] and which produces such bewildering results in Philo. Other features which distinguish the Gnostic systems from Plotinus are that in Valentinian Gnosticism, at all events, the production of the aeons is not necessary or eternal but dependent on the will of the First Principle;[3] and the sexuality, the wholesale transference of sexual desire to the spiritual world, which is characteristic at least of Simonian and Valentinian Gnosticism.[4] Among the Simonians a great part is played by the strange, typically Gnostic figure of the Prostitute who is also the Great Mother, on earth Helena;[5] while Valentinianism is a positive orgy of προυνικία, of abstract lusts and spiritual copulations.[6] From this Plotinus is utterly remote.[7]

[1] Cp. Lebreton, *Histoire du Dogme de la Trinité*, pp. 81–121, for a good short account of these systems. Good examples of their syncretistic character are the sudden appearance of the female Indefinite Dyad in the Valentinian system described in Hippolytus, *Philos.* VI. 29. 5–30, and the curious speculations about the Cross (the aeon Stauros or Horos) deriving from a Gnostic exegesis of Plato's account of the making of the World-Soul, *Tim.* 36 B (cp. Bousset, "Ps. Weltseele und das Kreuz Christi", *Zeitschr. für N.T. Wissensch.* vol. XIV, pp. 273–85).

[2] E.g. in Irenaeus's account of Basilides, *Advers. Haeres.* IV. 1. 24. 3, we find Phronesis, Sophia, Dynamis, etc. and Valentinian systems are full of similar names, cp. Hippol. *l.c.* and Ps.-Tertullian, 12.

[3] Hippol. *l.c.*

[4] Basilides, whose aeons are generated singly and not in couples like those of Valentinus (Iren. IV. 1. 24. 3), seems to have been fairly free from this sexuality.

[5] Justin, *Apol.* I. 26. 3; Iren. I. 23. 8 ff.

[6] Epiphan. *Haeres.* XXXI. 5.

[7] Though he often calls the One the Father, he prefers the light-metaphor to even that approach to the idea of physical generation.

4-2

The relation, or absence of relation, between Νοῦς in Plotinus and the Logos of Philo will be more conveniently discussed at a later stage in our examination. We can now proceed to discuss the doctrine of emanation. I desire to limit the use of this term strictly to that conception which is conveyed in the metaphor of radiation, for which it is perhaps the most convenient English term, though it does not represent exactly anything in the philosophical vocabulary of the *Enneads*. Its one disadvantage is that it may lead, and has led in the past, to confusion between the philosophy of Plotinus and that of others with whom he has nothing in common, and this possibility we have now disposed of.

It is fairly clear what Plotinus means to express in his account of emanation. Νοῦς and Ψυχή are produced by a spontaneous and necessary efflux of life or power from the One, which leaves their source undiminished. The relation between the One and Νοῦς is described as being like that of the sun and its light,[1] or in similes from the "radiative" effects of fire, snow, or perfumes.[2] The difficulty is, to give the conception any philosophical meaning. It is not easy to see what the significance of this conception of emanation or radiation can be when applied to two spiritual beings, and in particular how, if the process is necessary and eternal, the one can be inferior to the other or essentially different in character. The metaphor does not really work when applied to the peculiar relationship which must exist between the One and Νοῦς. We must, I think, admit if we read the passages in question that Plotinus is really trying to give an explanation of this relationship; he is not content simply to say that the One "produces" Νοῦς in some mysterious way which he is unable to define. His explanation, however, takes the form of a baffling and unsatisfactory metaphor. This is especially strange, because Plotinus is usually quite aware of the unsatisfactoriness of metaphors as a final form of philosophical exposition, and criticizes his own acutely.[3] We can, of course, bring forward general considerations which make the difficulty less

[1] I. 7. 1; V. 3. 12, 5. 8, 6. 4; VI. 8. 18, 9. 9. [2] V. 1. 2.

[3] E.g. in the discussion of the partibility of the soul at the beginning of IV. 3; cp. also the simile of the radii, VI. 5. 5.

formidable. We can say that this confusion of thought was the price which had to be paid to maintain the organic unity of the cosmos, an indispensable postulate alike of magic, Greek religion, and Greek philosophy. We can agree with Arnou[1] that every term in Plotinus's philosophical vocabulary brings a little piece of its parent system with it, that his tradition was too complex for him to master completely. That this is true can be seen clearly throughout the *Enneads*. It would, however, be satisfactory if we could make some approach to a more detailed solution. This it seems possible to do by investigating the past history of the conception of emanation, even if at first sight such an investigation only seems to make confusion worse confounded.

The first appearance of anything that can be called a theory of emanation in the Greek philosophical tradition is to be found in that later Stoicism which goes under the name of Posidonius.[2] It appears in the account of the history of the soul. The modifications which the divine substance endures in the cosmologies of the older Stoicism[3] have disappeared. We find a genuine emanation of the πνεῦμα νοερὸν καὶ πυρῶδες, the hegemonikon, from the sun,[4] combined with the distinctive theory of "undiminished giving" of light[5] which is the basis of Plotinus's light metaphor. The important thing to notice for the present purpose is that the theory is completely materialistic. What comes from the visible sun and returns to it again is a fiery breath. Given Stoic physics and Stoic materialism this idea of a material outflowing of the material hegemonikon is perfectly natural and in place; but it is by no means in place in an account of the relations between spiritual beings in the system of a thinker like Plotinus, who is very clear about the distinction between

[1] Pp. 62–3.

[2] Cp. Witt, "Plotinus and Posidonius", *C.Q.* vol. XXIV, 1930, p. 198, and especially pp. 205–7.

[3] Von Arnim, *St. Vet. Fragm.* I. 102, etc.

[4] Plutarch, *De Facie in Orbe Lunae*, 943 A ff. (mixed with a good deal of confused demonology); Galen, *De Plac.* 643 ff., Mueller; Macrobius, *Sat.* I. 23; Dodds, *Proclus, The Elements of Theology*, pp. 315–18; Reinhardt, *Kosmos und Sympathie*, pp. 353–65.

[5] Witt, *l.c.*

material and spiritual. Further, Plotinus is extremely conscious that materialism is the supreme defect of Stoic thought, and criticizes it vigorously.[1] The unsatisfactoriness of the concept of emanation, therefore, becomes even more marked when we realize that it involves a concealed admission of Stoic materialism into Plotinus's system.

The only investigation which seems to throw any light on how this came about is the following up of the history of a subsidiary doctrine vital to Plotinus's theory of emanation, that of the incorporeality of light.[2] If the passages in the *Enneads* in which this doctrine occurs are considered in chronological order it becomes apparent that it underwent a certain development, or at least modification, in Plotinus's mind. In the later treatises, II. 1 and IV. 5, we have simply the statement that light is incorporeal though dependent on body, an ἐνέργεια of body. In IV. 5. 6–7, this statement appears as a criticism of the Aristotelian doctrine[3] according to which light is also incorporeal, but is simply "a phenomenon in the diaphanous", the presence in it of the luminary source. Aristotle, while maintaining that light was not technically a σῶμα, regarded it simply as a physical phenomenon. Plotinus is concerned to give it a more august status. His own doctrine is doubtless dependent on the account of colour as a material ἀπορροή of particles given in the *Timaeus*[4] and is deeply affected by the Posidonian theory of light.[5] What seems to be his own is the combination of the doctrines that light is incorporeal and that it is the outflow of the luminary, and also the very close parallelism that he maintains exists between light and life, the Act or ἐνέργεια of the soul.[6] This last point should be noted, as it at once raises the status of light in the universe enormously. It is no longer a mere physical incident but a manifestation of the spiritual principle of reality or activity in the luminary, its λόγος or εἶδος.

In I. 6. 3 Plotinus goes even further than he does in the passages above referred to and says that light is itself λόγος and εἶδος, the principle of form in the material world. Moreover, he goes on to

[1] II. 4. 1. [2] II. 1. 7; IV. 5. 6, 7; I. 6. 3; Zeller, III. 2, p. 553 (4th ed.).
[3] *De An.* 418 A; Beare, *Greek Theories of Elementary Cognition*, pp. 57 ff.
[4] 67 D. [5] Witt, *l.c.* [6] IV. 5. 7; Julian, *Or.* IV. 133 D–134 A.

make the surprising statements that fire "holds the position of Form in relation to the other elements"[1] though itself a body, and that it is near to the incorporeal inasmuch as it is the subtlest of bodies, that the others receive it into themselves but it does not receive the others.[2] This would fit well enough in a Stoic, but it is startling to find it in Plotinus, even in an early treatise. The whole passage is on the border-line between Neo-Platonism and Stoicism. It combines the doctrine that there is no clear frontier between material and spiritual because the principle of reality even in material things is spiritual with the doctrine that there is no clear frontier because "spirit" is only the finest and subtlest form of matter.

This unguarded remark about the nature of fire is, I think, unparalleled in Plotinus. He is not usually in danger of lapsing into naïve confusions between matter and spirit. What is, however, clear from all the passages referred to above is that Plotinus, in asserting the incorporeality of light, does not simply mean like Aristotle to maintain that light is not a body but an incident of a body. He gives to light a very special status on the frontier of spirit and matter. This conclusion is supported by another passage[3] in which the same type of thought takes a rather different form. The eleventh chapter of the first treatise on the Problems of the Soul begins with an exposition of the doctrine of "appropriate physical receptacles" of soul. This is a further development of the doctrine of "analogy", of the exact correspondence of the visible and intelligible universe.[4] As applied here to the making of shrines and images[5] it implies that some physical bodies are naturally more receptive of soul than others. Plotinus then goes on to describe the connection between the world of Νοῦς and the sense-world in a way that gives a position of peculiar importance to the sun. Νοῦς is described—rather casually, as a παράδειγμα for the immediate purpose—by the image so often applied to the One, as "the sun of

[1] This of course is Pythagorean doctrine, which may have made Plotinus more ready to accept it. See Aristotle, *De Gen. et Corr.* 335a. 15 ff. Burnet, *Early Greek Philosophy*, p. 109.

[2] Cp. Julian, *Or.* IV. 141 C–D. [3] IV. 3. 11. [4] VI. 7. 6, 12.

[5] Cp. the more crudely magical but analogous idea of "making gods" in Asclepius, III, 23b–24d.

the other world", ὁ ἐκεῖ ἥλιος. The soul is said to be an intermediary, οἷον ἑρμηνευτική, between this sun of the other world and the visible sun. With this may be compared another passage[1] where "the visible gods as far as the moon", i.e. the sun and stars, are said to be related to the νοητοὶ θεοί as its radiance is to a star. Here we find not only light but the luminous bodies, and especially the sun, brought into especially close relation with the intelligible universe, standing on the frontiers of visible and invisible; a position which is confirmed in the case of the sun by the frequent use of the sun-metaphor for the One and, as here, for Νοῦς.

This peculiar position of the sun is of course well known in the later developments of Neo-Platonism, and is particularly characteristic of the theology of the Emperor Julian.[2] It is, however, interesting to discover traces of the "solar theology" in the works of a writer so independent of contemporary religious ideas as Plotinus, particularly as the passages in question occur in treatises[3] written apparently later than the penetrating criticism of this very theology of radiation contained in VI. 4 and 5.[4] No doubt Plotinus thought that he was simply following the teaching of Plato about the Sun in *Republic* VI–VII and was influenced in the working out of his theory by Plato's emphatic assertion of the divinity of the heavenly bodies in *Timaeus* 40B and still more in the *Laws* 821B, 898D f. The passages just quoted seem however to go beyond anything in Plato and to show distinct traces of contemporary influences. Their interest is still further enhanced by comparison with a passage in the *Hermetica* which may be roughly contemporary with Plotinus.[5] In this passage the light of the sun, source of all being and life in the visible world, is said to be the receptacle of νοητὴ οὐσία,[6] "but of what that substance consists or whence it flows God (or the sun)

[1] III. 5. 6.

[2] *Or.* IV. 132D–133, 135D, 139D–140A; *Or.* V. 172B–C. Cp. Macrobius, *Sat.* I. 23.

[3] IV. 3; III. 5. 27 and 26 in Porphyry's chronological order.

[4] 22 and 23 in Porphyry's chronological order.

[5] XVI. 6 (Scott). For commentary and discussion of date see Scott, *Hermetica*, vol. II, pp. 428 ff., also vol. I, Introd. p. 8.

[6] Cp. Julian, *Or.* V. 172B–C.

only knows". The Hermetic writer is rather clumsily trying to solve the problem created by the superimposition on the organic universe of the "Posidonian" solar theology of the Platonic intelligible universe, whose existence he rather grudgingly admits. This has points of contact with the problem which Plotinus is trying to solve by his theory of emanation. The solution, too, proposed by the Hermetist corresponds very closely with the doctrine of "appropriate physical receptacles" and the important place given to the sun in *Enneads*, IV. 3. 11.

I do not wish to suggest that Plotinus was influenced by Hermetic teaching, either through that unknown and probably unknowable intermediary the teaching of Ammonius Saccas or in any other way. Still less do I wish to suggest that Plotinus could at any period of his life have been called a "solar theologian" or a sun-worshipper. What does seem to be true is that he was familiar with a type of solar theory (perhaps partly his own invention) in which the sun's light was thought of either as the appropriate receptacle for the immaterial substance of the intelligible world, as the intermediary between material and spiritual, or as itself incorporeal, closely parallel to the life of soul, and again on the frontier of spiritual and material (this last form of the theory may be a refinement of Plotinus's own). Allied to the principle of "analogy"[1] this theory would provide very good ground for the growth of Plotinus's theory of emanation. Given that everything in the visible cosmos is an image of something in the intelligible, and that light is itself a spiritual energy or activity, what is more natural than to represent spiritual activity and productivity in terms of light? It would be much better suited to this purpose than the original "Posidonian" theory of the emanation of the fiery soul from the sun, the materialism of which would naturally repel Plotinus, and the influence of which is more clearly apparent in Neo-Platonic theories about πνεῦμα and astral bodies[2] than in the Plotinian theory of emanation itself. The theory of emanation expressed in the metaphor of radiation belongs to a type of thought in which there is a wide and doubtful borderland between matter and spirit. What seems to lie behind it is not simply the late Stoic theory

[1] VI. 7. 6, 12.

[2] Dodds, *Proclus*, pp. 315–18.

of an organic universe centring in the sun but an attempt to reconcile this theory with the Platonic conception of a hierarchy of reality, sensible and intelligible, through the mediation of a half-spiritual, half-material realm of light. This is the theory which we find in *Hermetica* XVI, and the passages which I have quoted seem to show that Plotinus knew it and found it acceptable. If this is really so, the theory of emanation by radiation would be one of the very few parts of Plotinus's philosophy which can be shown to be affected by contemporary philosophical and religious thought, to which he is generally remarkably superior. It is, perhaps, significant that this lapse from his usual clarity into a way of thinking more characteristic of his contemporaries, with their slipshod inaccuracy and reliance on the imagination rather than the reason, occurs in an attempt to maintain unbroken the organic unity of the cosmos, a postulate indispensable to all the non-Christian thought of the epoch, the foundation both of its magic and its religion.

As a pendant to this discussion of Plotinus's theory of emanation we must consider the nearest approach which he himself makes to a criticism of it. This is contained in the treatise VI. 4.[1] As the theory of emanation is always expressed in metaphorical terms, so the criticism of it takes the form of a very acute analysis of the metaphor. The criticism is, however, rather implicit than explicit, and Plotinus does not seem to have been altogether conscious of the very far-reaching consequences for his system which spring from this analysis and from others of the conclusions which he draws in this treatise and that which follows it.

The treatises VI. 4 and 5[2] appear to be concerned with the relation of Νοῦς, the ἓν ὄν or primary and authentic being, to Soul and the visible universe. They stand, however, rather apart from Plotinus's other writings about Νοῦς. They are dominated throughout by the doctrine of the "infinite self", of which they afford the most striking expressions.[3] As a result of the domination of this idea, the

[1] Ch. 7.

[2] Their title in Porphyry's edition, Περὶ τοῦ τὸ ὂν ἓν καὶ ταὐτὸν ἅμα πανταχοῦ εἶναι ὅλον πρῶτον.

[3] VI. 4. 14, 5. 7, 12.

insistence on the unity of Self and All and One, the distinction between Νοῦς the All or One-Being, and the One itself, seems at times almost to disappear. There is no trace of that sharp transcendence of the One, that insistence on its otherness from Νοῦς which appears in other parts of the *Enneads*.[1] Sometimes, as in the discussion of the "God within us" in the fourth chapter of the fifth treatise, it is difficult to see whether Νοῦς or the One is referred to. In the simile of the radii, too,[2] we seem to have, in the single centre in which all the generating centres of the radii coincide, an immanent One, unifying the One-Being, the "morphische Einheit" of Nebel. The real subject of the treatises seems to be the omnipresence of the fullness of unified real being which is also man's true self if he will only realize his greatness, and which centres on and is made one by the immanent One,[3] or in general the relation of spiritual unity to material multiplicity. Just as when the transcendence of the One is insisted on, as in VI. 8, it takes to itself some of the attributes of Νοῦς, so here, where it is the all-embracing unity of the spiritual world which is stressed, Νοῦς almost becomes the One, the supreme principle and highest stage of unity.[4]

It is against this background of thought, in which the normal distinctions which Plotinus makes within the spiritual world become less important, and our attention is concentrated on a simple contrast of spiritual unity and material multiplicity, that we must consider Plotinus's analysis of his metaphor of emanation. The passage is worth translating nearly in full. It runs: "If you take a small luminous mass as centre and surround it with a larger transparent sphere, so that the light within shows over the whole of that which surrounds it...shall we not say that the inner [luminous] mass is not affected in any way but remains in itself and reaches over the whole of the outer mass, and that the light which is seen in the little central

[1] III. 8. 8, 9; V. 4. 1, 3. 11; VI. 7. 26. [2] 5. 5. [3] 4. 11.

[4] Cp. 5. 9: εἴπερ οὖν ἀληθεύσει τὸ ἓν τοῦτο, καθ' οὗ δὴ καὶ κατηγορεῖν ἔστιν ὡς οὐσίαν τὸ ἕν, etc. Granted that Plotinus is here expounding the *Parmenides* and that his readers would be expected to understand that he was referring to the "second One" (see Bréhier's introduction to the treatises), we should expect more reference to the real "true One" of his system, the One above being.

body has encompassed the outer?...Now if one takes away the material mass and keeps the power of the light you cannot surely say that the light is anywhere any longer, but that it is equally distributed over the whole outer sphere; you can no longer determine in your mind where it was situated before, nor can you say whence it came nor how...but can only puzzle and wonder, perceiving the light simultaneously present throughout the sphere." Now it is clear that this elimination of the materialist element in the metaphor, the actual physical centre, has in effect destroyed the idea of emanation. The distinguishing characteristic of emanation is radiation from a centre. If the centre, as here, is removed, there can be no longer any question of emanation. What is left is simply an assertion of the omnipresence of the spiritual. In the same way his modifications of a too materialistic theory of the presence of the One-Being through its "powers",[1] his insistence that where the power is, there the source of the power must be present in all its fullness, that it is at once totally omnipresent and totally separate,[2] again lead to a destruction of any real idea of emanation. For it is substituted the doctrine of "reception according to the capacity of the recipient".[3] This, in a more developed form, appears as an alternative to emanation in Plotinus's account of the relation of Νοῦς to the One, and will have to be considered in more detail under the head of "Νοῦς as Mind". What it is important to see clearly at this stage is that, if the source is present in its fullness in the emanant, and the emanant is in no way less than the source, there can really be no true emanation at all—because there can be no real difference between source and emanant; and, in the same way, the doctrine that each thing participates in the One-Being according to its capacity removes the need for or possibility of a doctrine of emanation. The hold of the metaphor on Plotinus's mind must have been extraordinarily strong (due perhaps to the unique philosophical and religious position occupied for him, as for his predecessors and contem-

[1] δυνάμεις, 4. 3, 9 (the rejection of a too literal interpretation of the light metaphor according to which the emanant is less than that from which it emanates).

[2] E.g. Chs. 3, 8.

[3] Ch. 11.

poraries, by the sun and its light) for him to continue to use it without fully perceiving the destructive force of his own closer analysis.

We now come to a rather curious by-form or extreme development of the theory of emanation, in which the One is represented as a root or seed, the potentiality from which all things evolve into actuality. This comparison is often used by Plotinus to describe the relation of the lower hypostases to the higher.[1] The idea obviously, if pressed too far, would invert the whole system and transform it from an Aristotelian-Platonic metaphysic in which Act precedes potency into an evolutionary system of the type of the earlier Stoicism. In the passages which I particularly wish to consider this inversion seems actually to take place. The most complete expression of it is to be found in the very early and for the most part strongly Platonic treatise on the Descent of the Soul (IV. 8). In the fifth chapter of this treatise he states emphatically that the soul (from the context the human soul is meant) has potentialities which can only be actualized in the material world, and which would remain useless and undeveloped if the soul were to remain in the immaterial. The conception of a lower soul whose special task it is to organize matter is in itself not un-Plotinian, as we shall see later. It is, however, rather startling to find Plotinus asserting that the lower soul finds the fullness and perfection of its life in the lower, material, and not in the higher, spiritual world. At the beginning of Ch. 6, however, he goes even further. He says: "If then it is necessary that not only One should exist—for then all things would have been hidden in it and would have had no definite shape, nor would any of the real beings have existed if it had stayed still in itself, nor would there have been the multitude of these beings generated from the One, nor of those which take their outgoing after this multitude, which hold the rank of souls—in the same way it was also necessary that not only souls should exist, in the absence of those things which come into being through them; that is supposing that every nature

[1] E.g. III. 3. 7 (where the metaphor of the One as root is elaborately worked out); IV. 8. 5, 6 (applied to the One and to Soul); V. 9. 6 (applied to Νοῦς).

has this inherent quality of making that which comes after it and of unrolling itself as if proceeding from a sort of partless seed as a beginning to the perceptible end. The prior being remains always in its proper place, and that which comes after is as it were generated from an ineffable power [or potency]...." He then goes on to introduce the Platonic argument of the "ungrudgingness" of the higher being which causes it to diffuse itself in the production of the lower.

Plotinus here just saves himself from lapsing completely into the evolutionary pantheism of the Stoics by the phrase μένοντος μὲν ἀεὶ τοῦ προτέρου ἐν τῇ οἰκείᾳ ἕδρᾳ, but he comes nearer to it, I think, than in any other passage of his writings. We may compare that passage in the treatise *Against the Gnostics* where in his anxiety to maintain the excellence of the visible world against its detractors he is led into a rather similar inversion. "The Good will not be the Good, or Mind Mind, the Soul will not be itself unless some second life lives after the first...."[1] Plotinus is fond of the word ἐξελίττεσθαι, used in the first passage quoted, and uses it elsewhere of the Logoi. Here it and the comparison to a seed are applied to all the Hypostases, including the One itself. We have here expressed the conception of the evolution from the One to the sense-world as an evolution from potency to act, a passage to a greater fullness and extent of being. This, of course, is the exact opposite of Plotinus's real thought about the relation of the two. I do not believe that Plotinus ever really regarded the One as potency and the material world as act. If we were to interpret the passage quoted in this sense we should both be ignoring its own qualifications and limitations and setting up an impossible contradiction to the rest of the *Enneads*. He has, however, gone far enough in this direction to betray himself into serious inconsistency. The One may be the beginning of all things, but it cannot really for Plotinus be a spermatic beginning. In his normal teaching the potentialities of each hypostasis are actualized not by the production of what is below it but by the contemplation of what is above it.[2] His system is teleological rather than evolutionary, the beginning is the End,

[1] II. 9. 3.

[2] Cp. especially II. 4. 5; V. 2.

the Cause of Being, which is above actuality, not below it. The main thrust, the direction of the universal forces, is upwards and inwards, not downwards and outwards. For all that Plotinus has to account for the existence of the Beings below the One. It remains to consider why in this early attempt to do so he was led into so great an inconsistency with the Platonic-Aristotelian tradition and his own real thought.

The most obvious and immediate, and undoubtedly the true, source of this "spermatic" doctrine of the One is the Stoic idea of the σπέρμα, or σπερματικὸς λόγος,[1] and especially that form of it in which God is spoken of as the σπέρμα or λόγος σπερματικός of the universe.[2] In the hylozoist Stoic system with its biologico-physical "living and intelligent fire", such a conception was natural enough. It is particularly characteristic of the earlier Stoicism, with its cyclic modifications of the divine substance. Plotinus's passionate desire to maintain the organic unity of the cosmos is the element in his thought which brings him closest to the Stoics; we have already seen[3] how this results in the admission of concealed Stoic materialism into his system in the theory of emanation. Here we have a more extreme example of the same thing, an inversion of values which seems to involve (though Plotinus never explicitly says so) the regarding of the visible cosmos as the flowering and perfection, the realization of the dormant potentialities, of the One. This is excellent Stoicism; for to the Stoics the visible cosmos was the highest perfection of being and the object of a genuinely religious devotion. It is, however, by no means good Platonism or Neo-Platonism.

There is a subsidiary reason which would have made it easier for Plotinus to slide into the "spermatic" view of the evolution of the universe from the One. This is the extreme of negation to which he sometimes goes in speaking of his First Principle. It is interesting to note that Speusippus, whose influence on the extreme form of the "negative theology" of Plotinus was, as we have seen,[4] considerable

[1] S.V.F. II. 596, 618, 1027; Marc. Aurel. IX. 1; Sen. *Ep.* 90. 29, etc.

[2] S.V.F. I. 102 (Zeno); II. 580.

[3] Above, pp. 53 ff.

[4] Above, pp. 17–19, 21–23.

though indirect, also calls his One a σπέρμα.[1] There does not seem here to be any question of a continuing tradition, or of anything more than a coincidence, though it is a coincidence which illustrates a point of contact in the thought of the two philosophers. Any possibility of a continued survival in the thought of the Christian era of the evolutionary mathematical metaphysic of the Pythagoreans, which Speusippus adopted, would seem to be eliminated by the fact that the primal One is not spermatic in the later Pythagorean tradition, as represented by the passages previously quoted from Eudorus, pseudo-Brotinus, and Moderatus.[2]

[1] Ar. *Met.* Λ, 7. 1072b; N, 5. 1092a.

[2] Ch. II, pp. 22–23.

CHAPTER V

ΝΟΥΣ AS MIND AND WORLD

THE next aspect of Νοῦς which must be considered is the psychological, Νοῦς as mind. As the retention of so traditional a name shows, this is in a sense the most primitive and fundamental aspect of Plotinus's complex conception. It is certainly that aspect of the Second Hypostasis which links on most clearly to earlier thought. We have seen already how Aristotle's conception of a divine self-thinking mind standing at the head of the cosmic system entered among the Middle Platonists into somewhat uneasy relations with fragments of Plato's teaching and in particular interpretations of the *Timaeus* and *Parmenides*, together with Xenocrates's doctrine of a supreme mind-monad; and how elements of this confused tradition passed into Plotinus's doctrine of the One. The separation of the supreme principle into two, Νοῦς and that which transcends it, resulted in important modifications of the conception of Νοῦς as mind, due to the need of bringing it into relation with the One. In order to understand these modifications rightly, we must examine the part played in Plotinus's system by the conception of "spiritual ὕλη" or the Indefinite Dyad. The Indefinite Dyad derives, of course, from Plato,[1] and occurs frequently in post-Platonic Pythagoreanism.[2] It is not possible or important to enquire exactly where Plotinus got it from. It was part of the common Platonic-Pythagorean tradition which he inherited. It is worth noticing, however, that the passage quoted from Alexander Polyhistor shows that by the first century B.C. the Indefinite Dyad was regarded by the Pythagoreans as subordinate to and proceeding from the primal

[1] Cp. *Philebus*, 23 C ff., with what Aristotle says of his later teaching in *Met.* A, 6. 987b. 20 ff.

[2] Diog. Laert. VIII. 25 (quoting Alexander Polyhistor); Sext. *Adv. Math.* 10. 277; Hippol. *Refut.* I. 8; Simplicius, *Phys.* 36. 181. 7 D (the Eudorus passage before quoted).

monad. This is Plotinus's doctrine, but not apparently that of Plato, for whom the two principles seem to be independent correlatives, though not co-equal. It seems doubtful, however, whether this modification is really the result of Stoic influence,[1] though in the Sextus Empiricus passage[2] Stoic terms are used in speaking of the two principles (ἐν ταῖς ἀρχαῖς ταύταις τὸν μὲν τοῦ δρῶντος αἰτίου λόγον ἐπέχειν τὴν μονάδα, τὸν δὲ τῆς πασχούσης ὕλης τὴν δυάδα). It is more likely that what we have here (in the Alexander passage) is an example of that type of system headed by a "positive" Xenocratean monad[3] which I have discussed in my earlier chapters.

Plotinus's doctrine of "spiritual ὕλη" results from a combining of the traditional presentation of the Indefinite Dyad with Aristotle's doctrine of ὕλη as pure potency. This last usually enters into Plotinus's thought through Aristotle's application of it in the *De Anima* to the thinking or perceiving subject. There is, however, one passage in the *Enneads* where we meet with a different application of the Peripatetic doctrine of ὕλη. This is the treatise *On the Two Kinds of Matter*,[4] the first five chapters of which, after a brief historical introduction, are devoted to the question of "matter" in the spiritual or intelligible world. The treatise follows Aristotle more closely than is usual in the *Enneads*.[5] In the fourth chapter the "intelligible ὕλη" is presented as the common substrate which is informed and differentiated by the εἴδη, the necessary and only mentally separable correlative of form, which must be found wherever there are forms, in the intelligible world as well as the world of sense. This account which makes of the intelligible world simply a duplicate of the Aristotelian sense-world,[6] with the differences as regards permanence expounded in Chs. 3 and 5, is difficult to reconcile with Plotinus's ordinary account of the world of Νοῦς. Νοῦς here does not seem to function as Mind, and the conception of the interpenetrability of the intellectual-intelligible

[1] Ueberweg–Praechter, p. 517. [2] *Adv. Math.* 10. 277.

[3] Cp. *Plac.* I. 7; *Dox.* 302 (the monad = θεός and νοῦς).

[4] II. 4. [5] Cp. Bréhier's introduction to the treatise.

[6] Notice the argument that "because there is matter here, there must be matter There, since this cosmos is an image of That", which is very characteristic of one aspect of Plotinus's thought.

beings is absent. The principle of unity in the intelligible world is simply its matter. This is not only difficult to fit in with Plotinus's general thought. It is also difficult to reconcile with the next chapter (5) of the same treatise. Plotinus has already in Ch. 3 suggested the normal function of the concept of ὕλη in the intelligible world when he speaks of the unformed offering itself to that which is above it to receive form, and gives the relations of Soul and Νοῦς as an instance. He now, at the end of Ch. 5, gives an account of the origin of matter in the intelligible world according to which it is eternally generated from the First, produced by "otherness" which is "the first movement". This "movement" or "otherness", the outgoing of Νοῦς from the One, is ἀόριστος until it returns upon the One and is informed or delimited (ὁρίζεται) by it. It is itself dark but is illuminated by the First, which is other than it. Here we have obviously returned from Aristotle to Plato; much of the language which Plotinus uses is clearly derived direct from the *Sophist* or the *Philebus*. There is perhaps one trace of the confusion caused by the introduction of Aristotelian ideas in the preceding chapter. We should expect, from other similar passages, to find it said that the Ideas are produced by the return of the Indefinite upon the One.[1] Instead, the Ideas or forms and ὕλη are simply spoken of as both generated from the First, and we are left to assume that their relation to each other is that indicated in the previous chapter. Thus we have the ὕλη of the intelligible world informed at once by the forms and by the One. This apparent incompatibility could be resolved by adopting the doctrine fully stated in VI. 7 and V. 3 (of which I shall have more to say later), which is also hinted at in V. 4[2] and V. 1,[3] that the Ideas are generated because Νοῦς, in its return upon the One in contemplation, perceives it as a multiplicity. This doctrine, however, though the remark in V. 4 suggests that it is contemporary with or earlier than *The Two Kinds of Matter*, will not altogether enable us to reconcile with Plotinus's normal thought

[1] Cp. V. 1. 5, 4. 2.

[2] V. 4. 2: καὶ πολλὰ ὁρῶν ἤδη (of Νοῦς contemplating the One).

[3] V. 1. 5, where the text is corrupt but it is clear that Plotinus is stating that in one sense Νοῦς is informed by the One, in another by "number" or the Ideas.

the representation of the Ideas as principles of division and multiplicity in Νοῦς and "matter" as a principle of unity. What we seem to have here is an unsuccessful attempt to adopt the Aristotelian doctrine of form and matter without properly adapting it to the requirements of the system. Plotinus seems to have realized the unsatisfactoriness of the position, for in the rather later treatise II. 5 in which the subject of Potency and Act is discussed, though he retains his own characteristic doctrine of "spiritual ὕλη",[1] the orthodox Peripatetic argumentation of II. 4. 4 does not reappear.

In the passages quoted from the Fifth Ennead[2] there is also no trace of Aristotelian hylomorphism. What we have is simply an explanation of Plato's "unlimited" or Indefinite Dyad and "principle of limit" in terms of Aristotle's psychology. Through his equation of the actualization of the mind by that which it thinks with the delimiting and information of the Indefinite Dyad by the One Plotinus is able to provide a more satisfactory account of the relations of the One and Νοῦς than the metaphorical theory of emanation. It is true that the first stage in the eternal cyclic process, the original movement of the "formless" Νοῦς from the One, remains an emanation of a rather undefined sort; and because of this Plotinus is enabled to give both accounts simultaneously without any sense of incongruity between them.[3] The "psychological" account of the inter-relation of the two hypostases does, however, provide a valuable reinforcement at one of the weakest points of the system.

We have already glanced at one difficulty involved in this doctrine. For Plotinus the content of Νοῦς is not the One but the multiplex unity of the νοητά. Yet the informing principle of Νοῦς, and the primary object of its contemplation, is the One. How are these two positions to be reconciled? We can leave aside the "mystical" doctrine that Νοῦς apprehends the One by that in it which is not Νοῦς,[4] by forsaking or transcending its own nature and intellectual

[1] Cp. II. 5. 3.

[2] V. 4. 2; V. 1. 5.

[3] Cp. the transition from one idea to the other in V. 1. 5–6, and their juxtaposition in V. 2. 1.

[4] V. 5. 8.

powers, and casting itself upon the One in an act of love.[1] What we are dealing with here is that more normal and constant contemplation by which Νοῦς is itself. We have seen that in v. 1 and v. 4 Plotinus is conscious of the difficulty and suggests its solution. In vi. 7,[2] a work of his middle period, and in the very late treatise v. 3[3] he gives us a full exposition of the subtle doctrine by which he overcomes it. In both these treatises, particularly the latter, the transcendence and separateness of the One is stressed and the "multiple" element in Νοῦς is insisted upon. In vi. 7. 15 Νοῦς is said to derive its power to generate the multiplicity of the Ideas from the One. The multiplicity "comes to it from the One". It is unable to keep the power it acquires from the One in its original state and so breaks it up (ἣν γὰρ ἐκομίζετο δύναμιν ἀδυνατῶν ἔχειν συνέθραυε καὶ πολλὰ ἐποίησε τὴν μίαν, ἵν' οὕτω δύναιτο κατὰ μέρος φέρειν).

The process is described in rather more detail in v. 3. This treatise is a product of Plotinus's extreme old age, and is marked by an unusual sharpness in the lines of separation drawn between the different hypostases, and especially by an insistence on the otherness of the human soul, even at its highest, from Νοῦς and the One. The distinction between these last two is also stressed as strongly as anywhere in the *Enneads*. In consequence in the eleventh chapter we have a very detailed account of the information of Νοῦς by the One. The return of Νοῦς upon its source is described as consisting of two stages. In the first it tries to apprehend the One in its simplicity, it moves towards it as "sight no longer seeing", but in the second stage, so far from apprehending the One in its simplicity it is ἄλλο ἀεὶ λαμβάνων ἐν αὑτῷ πληθυνόμενον, it "comes out holding that which itself has multiplied". The "mystical" union of Νοῦς and the One does not appear. We know however from vi. 7[4] that it is something other than this normal pluralizing contemplation; it is an act in which Νοῦς becomes unified by transcending itself. In the account, however, of the normal mode in which Νοῦς contemplates

[1] vi. 7. 35. [2] Ch. 15. [3] Ch. 11.

[4] Ch. 35. This chapter suggests that the primal "movement" of Νοῦς towards the One is to be identified with the mystical contemplation, καὶ γὰρ ὁρῶν ἐκεῖνον ἔσχε γεννήματα καὶ συνῄσθετο καὶ τούτων γενομένων καὶ ἐνόντων κ.τ.λ.

the One which has just been given we have the solution of our difficulty. The Forms, number, the internal multiplicity of the One-Being, are the way in which the One is apprehended by and informs Νοῦς. The incurable multiplicity of the Divine Mind causes the One itself to be mirrored in it, not in its own simplicity, but as multiform.

Can the origin of this conception be found simply in Plotinus's invariable statement that intellection involves multiplicity, at least the duality of subject and object, from which he deduces the necessity of the transcendent One above Νοῦς?[1] I do not think so, because after all the problem is a different one. Plotinus is not trying to explain the origin of the distinction between Νοῦς and νοητόν but the multiplicity of the Forms, a multiplicity on which he insists, as it is necessary to the completeness of the Ideal universe. The problem is that of the development of multiplicity from absolute unity, and the method of solution proposed is through the inability of the contemplating mind to reproduce the absolute unity in itself. It is interesting to find a similar solution, though in a very different setting, in Philo's account of the "multiple" apparition of God to the human intellect, which occurs in his exegesis of the appearance of the Three Men to Abraham (in the *De Abrahamo* and the *Quaestiones in Genesim*). In the *De Abrahamo*[2] the resemblance to Plotinus is less striking. When the soul, Philo says, is illuminated by God she sees him as triple, one with a double shadow, which is the two greatest of the Powers, the creative and the royal; or, a little further on, alternatively and not very consistently, he says that the soul at the highest point of her contemplation sees God as one; but when she is "celebrating the lesser mysteries", and has not attained to the height of contemplation, she perceives him as triple, for she sees him not as he is in himself but in his works, as creating or ruling. There is, however, a passage in the *Quaestiones in Genesim*[3] which comes much closer to Plotinus. Here Philo says that the mind "sees God triple" owing to the weakness of its vision; "just as the bodily eye sees a double appearance from one light, so

[1] VI. 7. 37. [2] 121 ff. (Cohn-Wendland).
[3] IV. 8 (Aucher).

the eye of the soul, since it cannot apprehend the one as one, makes a triple perception, according to the appearances of the chief serving powers which stand beside the one".

There is, of course, nothing in Plotinus which corresponds to Philo's doctrine of the Powers; nor is there any trace in these passages of Philo of Plotinus's doctrine of the information of the mind by that which is above it; Philo, too, is speaking of the human, not the universal mind. When every allowance has been made, however, for the great divergences of the two contexts there does seem to be a real resemblance in the fundamental idea, that the mind grasps the supreme principle in multiplicity because it is incapable of apprehending its absolute unity.

This conclusion is to some extent supported by the fact that at this point in the system, the relation of Νοῦς as mind, or of the human mind when it has reached the Νοῦς level, to the One, there is a closer similarity to be seen between the thought of Plotinus and Philo than can be detected at any other point in the system. Professor Dodds,[1] it is true, makes an attempt to differentiate their doctrines of "ecstasy", that is, of the last stage in the ascent to the One from that which lies immediately below it. There is no doubt that in general Philo gives a very different picture of the relations of the soul to God from that given by Plotinus. The utter unlikeness of God to all created beings,[2] and his complete inaccessibility to the human reason[3] are emphasized by Philo in a way and for reasons entirely foreign to Plotinus. There is nothing in Plotinus either which corresponds to Philo's description of prophecy.[4] The difference here however is perhaps more in Philo's account of the results of the divine inspiration than in his conception of the inspiration itself, the possession of the prophet by the Divine power. For Plotinus the entrance of the One into the soul is an incommunicable and isolated experience. It has no physical or external consequences, or if it has he does not trouble to describe

[1] "The *Parmenides* of Plato and the Neo-Platonic One", *C.Q.* vol. XXII, 1928, p. 142.

[2] *De Somn.* I. 73; *Leg. Alleg.* II. I.

[3] *De Mut. Nom.* 7.

[4] Cp. Bréhier, *Idées Philosophiques et Religieuses de Philon*, pp. 174–96.

them. For Philo the entrance of God into the soul of the prophet results in the utterance of prophecies and is accompanied or preceded by physical and emotional disturbances which he describes minutely.[1] In their description of the normal life of the soul outside the supreme mystical experience the two differ even more widely. Philo is full of a deep humility towards God. He fears and loves Him as conscious of his own nothingness.[2] In this he belongs entirely to the Jewish tradition. Plotinus on the other hand has to the full the self-confidence of the Greek philosopher in the presence of the Divine.[3] Even his tremendous self-confidence, however, falters when it comes to the supreme mystical union. It is for this reason that I am inclined to regard the distinction which Dodds makes between him and Philo as too sharp. He says: "The Plotinian ecstasy, unlike the Philonic, is achieved by a sustained intellectual effort from within, and not by a denial of the reason or by a magical intervention from without; it is presented less as the abnegation of self-hood than as the supreme self-realization." We have already seen[4] that the number of passages in the *Enneads* where Plotinus speaks of the union with the One as the supreme self-realization without any qualification is very small, and there are other passages with a very different significance. In VI. 7. 35 τὸ νοεῖν is opposed most sharply to the ecstasy in which Νοῦς has the vision of the One. Νοῦς in the ecstasy is no longer ἔμφρων, but ἐρῶν and so ἄφρων, "drunk with nectar". ὁ δὲ ἔχει τὸ νοεῖν ἀεί, ἔχει δὲ καὶ τὸ μὴ νοεῖν, ἀλλὰ ἄλλως ἐκεῖνον βλέπειν.[5] In the treatise *On Contemplation* we have the same insistence that to attain to the contemplation of the One the intelligence must retire into the background, must cease to be altogether an intelligence.[6] Further, not only are intellection or rational knowledge and the mystical contemplation or union with the One sharply opposed to each other by Plotinus; the part played by the soul in attaining to the mystical union is sometimes repre-

[1] *De Ebriet.* 146–8; *De Gigant.* 44.

[2] *Quis rer. divin. heres sit*, 1–30, especially 22–30.

[3] Cp. Porphyry, *Vita Plotini*, Ch. 10.

[4] Above, Ch. III.

[5] Cp. the difficult passage in VI. 7. 16, where in the activity of Νοῦς "living" (the union with the One) seems to be opposed to "seeing".

[6] III. 8. 9.

sented as a purely passive one. The soul waits, conscious that all effort of its own is useless, for the sudden Presence, the entrance of the One which fills and illuminates the soul.[1] All this is strikingly like the account of the ecstasy given by Philo in the passage quoted by Dodds: "When the intelligence shines all around us, pouring as it were a noonday beam into the whole soul, we are in ourselves and not possessed, but when it comes to set, naturally ecstasy and the divine possession and madness fall upon us. For when the divine light shines, the human light sets, and when the divine light sets, the human dawns and rises.... It is not lawful for mortal and immortal to dwell together."[2] For Plotinus, too, when the "positive", transcendent aspect of the One is uppermost in his mind, the mystical union is something irrational and destructive of the normal life of intellection. It is "drunkenness"[3] and at least very much more like the state of οἱ ἐνθουσιῶντες καὶ κάτοχοι γενόμενοι than it is like any normal way of knowing by the reason.[4] This way of thinking does not imply either in Plotinus or in Philo any despising of the intellect. All that they assert is that the very rare state of mystical contemplation is not continuous with the intellectual life and can be spoken of as opposed to it. Both are developing the teaching of the *Phaedrus* and the *Symposium*.[5] It is interesting, however, to find two men so different in the general lines of their religious and philosophical thought developing it on this point so much in the same way. It is difficult to discover any connection between them except in the nature of the mystical experience itself and in the Greek tradition of the philosophical importance of ecstasy or enthusiasm which they both inherit. Demonstrable historical connection there is none. Numenius cannot be the connecting link either for the doctrine of the mystical union or for the doctrine of the normal pluralizing contemplation of the divine unity by the intellect; for his fragments show no traces of mystical devotion, and his Second Mind is pluralized through its contact

[1] V. 5. 8; V. 3. 17.
[2] *Quis rer. divin. heres sit*, 264–5.
[3] VI. 7. 35.
[4] V. 3. 14.
[5] The belief in the philosophical importance of ἐνθουσιασμός is a thoroughly Hellenic one, and goes back well before Plato, cp. A. Delatte, *Les Conceptions de l'Enthousiasme chez les Philosophes Présocratiques*.

with the visible world, not through its contemplation of the First.[1] All we can say is that the twofold similarity at this particular point in the two systems in the accounts of the mystical union and of the pluralizing contemplation of the divine principle by the intellect in its normal state does suggest more strongly than anything else in the *Enneads* an influence of Philo on Plotinus. Of course the scope of this influence, if it does exist, is strictly limited. Its most important effect is to provide Plotinus with a means of uniting Platonic-Pythagorean ideas about the generation of number with the conception of Νοῦς as contemplating Mind.

To complete this account of the relation of Νοῦς as Mind to the One it only remains to add that in this aspect Νοῦς is really prior to the νοητά.[2] The Ideas are produced by the intellectual activity of Νοῦς in contemplating the One. It may be said in general that whenever the relation of Νοῦς to the One is in question it is the "intellectual" aspect of the second hypostasis, Νοῦς as mind, which is predominant, even where it is not made so clearly prior to the νοητά as in the passages we have been considering. This is due to the fact that the One, when considered in its relation to Νοῦς, is for Plotinus the primary νοητόν,[3] the especial object of the contemplation of Νοῦς. When we turn to consider the relation of Νοῦς to the visible universe we find that, though the νοητά are certainly never prior to Νοῦς, they become of predominant importance, and Νοῦς as mind falls relatively into the background. There is really no function that it can perform with regard to the lower world. It does not think or organize the entities of the visible cosmos, and could not do so without trespassing on the territory of Soul.

It is not my intention in this study of the structure of Plotinus's system to devote more attention to the inner life of the Hypostases "themselves by themselves" than is necessary for the understanding of their relations with each other. Thus I shall only try to deal with the doctrine of "spiritual interpenetration" in relation to the concept of Νοῦς as world, as the truly organic universe which is the

[1] Fr. 26.

[2] As it is sometimes elsewhere in the *Enneads*, cp. v. 8. 12, where it "generates" the Forms.

[3] v. 4. 2, 6. 2.

archetype of the visible universe,[1] or the realm in which the human soul finds itself truly at home.[2] It is only as archetypal universe that Νοῦς can be said to have much relation with the visible universe in Plotinus's system. The work of ordering and governing this lower cosmos falls on the universal or higher soul, which I propose to discuss later. This "higher soul" is the nearest representative in Plotinus of the "second god" of Numenius[3] and also of the "mind of the whole heaven" of Albinus.[4] We have already seen[5] how a historical origin for the "positive" aspect of the One of Plotinus can be found in certain characteristics of the "first god" or supreme principle of these writers, notably in its identification with the "good beyond being" of the *Republic*[6] and the application to it of the negations of the First One of the *Parmenides*.[7] This must not, however, be allowed to disguise the fact that it is the Νοῦς of Plotinus, not the One, which corresponds and is intended to correspond with the supreme Νοῦς of earlier writers. Plotinus's frequent criticism of Aristotle for placing a self-thinking mind at the head of the universal order would alone make this clear. In trying to produce a picture of the universal order which would satisfy his very acute intellect and correspond with his experience he made a division of the confused mass of attributes, intelligence, transcendence of being, priority to the Ideas, etc. which earlier thinkers had applied to their first principle. He applied some of them to Νοῦς, some to the One; but the division which he made between these two Hypostases by no means corresponds to that between the first and second gods of the Middle Platonists. Their second principle is ψυχή rather than Νοῦς in any Plotinian sense, and it is with the ψυχή of Plotinus that it must be equated.

The relations of this higher ψυχή to Νοῦς do not require very detailed treatment, as they do not involve any great modification in the character of Νοῦς as already described. It is interesting to note that in many passages the relation of ψυχή to Νοῦς is exactly parallel

[1] VI. 7. 12; V. 1. 4, 8. 3, 4.

[2] E.g. VI. 3. 1; VI. 9. 9 (where the soul abides in the realm of Νοῦς while contemplating the One); IV. 8. 3.

[3] Fr. 25.

[4] *Didaskalikos*, Ch. 10.

[5] Ch. 1.

[6] Numenius, 10. 25.

[7] *Didaskalikos*, Ch. 10.

to that of Νοῦς to the One. Νοῦς is the source of what is good, beautiful and intelligent in the soul.[1] Soul is an emanant of Νοῦς, and its emanation is described in exactly the same metaphor of radiation which is used for the emanation of Νοῦς from the One.[2] Soul acts as matter and Νοῦς as form;[3] or Soul receives Νοῦς in proportion to its capacity.[4] In all the passages where the relation of the two is conceived in these ways, in terms of separateness and dependence, the aspect of Νοῦς as thinking mind is in the background. It is either the primary object of Soul's cognition or the giver of intelligence. In fact it is a duplicate of the One. The tension between the two types of thought, one showing an ordered hierarchic world of sharply separated hypostases and the other the "infinite self" to which no bounds can be put and which is identical with the All,[5] is very marked at this point in the system, as we can see by comparing the account given of the dignity and capacities of the human soul in v. i. 11, vi. 4 and 5 or vi. 9 with that in v. 3.

The conception of Νοῦς as the "god", the ruling and formative principle of soul, is connected with that of Νοῦς as the archetypal world, the universe of real being, by the presentation of Soul as a rightful inhabitant of the world of Νοῦς, though occupying the lowest rank in that world.[6] (Plotinus always prefers to represent the higher being metaphorically as containing the lower, being present *to* it as an all-embracing universe or atmosphere rather than *in* it.) The soul, however, is the only entity which inhabits both worlds, the world of Νοῦς and the visible universe. The other things in the visible universe are represented in the intelligible world by their archetypes or Ideas. In the presentation of this archetypal world Plotinus is to some extent original, though his originality results from the combination of pre-existing traditions.

Plotinus's description of the universe of Νοῦς has as obvious and genuine a Platonic foundation as any part of the *Enneads*. If we turn to the description of the model used by the Demiurge in the

[1] v. 3. 3, 4, 6, 8. 3. [2] E.g. v. 3. 9. [3] ii. 4. 3.
[4] vi. 4. 11. [5] See above, Ch. iii.
[6] iv. 8. 7. Here v. 3. 3, in accordance with the general tendency of that treatise, seems to mark a lowering of the status of the soul.

Timaeus[1] we shall find all the elements of the picture of the intelligible world drawn so elaborately and imaginatively by Plotinus in the treatise *On how the Multiplicity of the Forms came to be, and on the Good*,[2] except for the Νοῦς-νοητά relationship, which is necessarily post-Aristotelian. The *Timaeus* gives us the completeness and all-embracingness of the Ideal Universe,[3] its livingness, so strongly insisted on by Plotinus, its eternal and unchanging character. The clearly Platonic and Aristotelian origins of the doctrine of the Intelligible Universe make less likely Theiler's view that in the Intelligible universe of Plotinus we have simply the organic universe of Posidonius removed to a higher plane.[4] The most notably "Posidonian" passages in Plotinus for Theiler are the early chapters of VI. 7 and those parts of the second treatise *On the Problems of the Soul*, which deal with the soul of the earth and the universal sympathy in the visible universe.[5] With regard to these last, Theiler must be admitted to have proved his case. There certainly lies behind them a Stoicism of the later type, with its conception of the universal organism. With the world of Νοῦς, however, the case is different.

There may possibly be some Stoic influence shown in the emphasis on the single, all-pervading life[6] of the intelligible universe, but the basic idea comes from the *Timaeus*; and, if reinforcement for its Platonic origin be required, we can find it in the famous passage of the *Sophist*[7] where it is insisted that real being must have "motion and life and soul and mind".[8] The idea that the earth is alive and organic and that the other elements are in some sense alive[9] is

[1] 30–31. [2] VI. 7. 1–13.

[3] Plotinus repeats Plato's classification of the living creatures it contains, e.g. V. 1. 4.

[4] W. Theiler, *Vorbereitung des Neu-Platonismus*, Ch. II: "Plotin und Poseidonios". Cp. Reinhardt, *Kosmos und Sympathie*, especially pp. 115–20.

[5] IV. 4. 26, 31 ff. [6] VI. 7. 9, etc. [7] 248 E–249.

[8] This passage of the *Sophist* is clearly referred to in the discussion of the motion of Νοῦς, VI. 7. 13, especially in the passage beginning ἀλλὰ τί τὸ σεμνόν. From the *Sophist* too, probably (254 D–E), rather than from the account of the making of the world-soul in the *Timaeus*, come the ταὐτόν and ἕτερον of this chapter, as often elsewhere in Plotinus. V. 1. 4, 8. 4.

[9] VI. 7. 11.

Posidonian.[1] It is important however to notice that it is not principally on this argument that Plotinus relies to demonstrate that his world of Νοῦς is alive and organic, but on the argument that the archetypal elements must in virtue of their very place in that higher universe be full of life;[2] or that everything There, including the Forms of animals and plants, is λόγος, νοῦς and νόησις as well as ζωή. The "organic" character of the intelligible universe, its unity-in-diversity, the interdependence of whole and parts, do not depend for Plotinus on any Stoic theories about the vitality of seemingly inorganic matter or the "sympathy" existing between the different parts of the visible universe. He accepts them as true in their proper place, as applying to this world perceptible by the senses and as making the existence of an archetypal world of Νοῦς more easily credible. But the principle on which that world is organized as a unity-in-diversity is a psychological one, that of "spiritual interpenetration". Whether we consider the relations of the parts to each other and to the whole or of Νοῦς as a whole to the νοητά as a whole the intelligible universe of Plotinus is always a universe of minds and in a mind; and these minds are conceived in terms of the Aristotelian psychology, not of Stoic hylozoism. Νοῦς and its object are there the same, two aspects of one entity;[3] the mind is what it thinks;[4] in the same way the part is in a sense the whole because it is νοῦς and νόησις and so contains the whole by comprehending it, as the whole Νοῦς does.[5] Νοῦς cannot be cut up into parts and its world cannot be one of entities clearly separated as they are in space and time. It is one of Plotinus's greatest advances in thought that he saw more clearly than any of his predecessors that separation and distinctness, as we usually conceive them, are essentially bound up with matter, space and time.[6] Difference of essence or quality in an immaterial world does not exclude, and in fact demands, co-presence[7] and interpenetrability of the different entities.

[1] Witt, "Plotinus and Posidonius", *C.Q.* vol. XXIV, 1930, p. 205.
[2] Ch. 12; V. 8. 3–4; everything There, even earth, is οὐρανός; cp. VI. 2. 8.
[3] VI. 7. 9; V. 5. 1–2.
[4] Cp. *De An.* III. 4. 429b–430a.
[5] VI. 7. 9; VI. 4. 14; VI. 5. 6, 7, 12.
[6] E.g. VI. 4. 4.
[7] VI. 4. 11; 5. 4.

There are certainly "Posidonian" Stoic elements present in Plotinus's account of the world of Νοῦς. The most important which I have not already discussed are the conception of man as a "bridge-being" on the frontiers of the higher and lower worlds,[1] the adoption of the "Posidonian" scale of unity[2] (adapted to fit the Plotinian hierarchy of hypostases and view of the sense-world), and the acceptance of Forms of individuals,[3] which derives from the Stoic doctrine of the ἰδίως ποιόν.[4] The first of these is not of great importance in a consideration of the "organic" quality of the intelligible world, though it may well be one of the sources of Plotinus's characteristic conception of the human soul as without clear bounds or frontiers, ranging over the whole of his system. The second, the adoption by Plotinus of Posidonius's scale of unity, is, I think, of less significance in general and in particular of less relevance in connection with the world of Νοῦς than some students of the relation between the two systems have made out. There is no One in Posidonius's system and neither is there a One-and-Many or unity-in-diversity in the sense in which those words are used of Νοῦς by Plotinus, whether he is thinking of it as the One-Being, the second One of the *Parmenides*, or as the unity-in-multiplicity of the Forms. Plotinus's use, therefore, of the Stoic scale of unity is like his use of the doctrine of the aliveness of seemingly inorganic things like the elements. It provides him with a useful argument to support his own teaching in discussion with people habituated to Stoic ways of thinking. It does not add anything important to his system, and so does not represent any important influence of Posidonius or of later Stoicism in general on him.

The third point, the acceptance of Forms of individuals, is of more importance. It is worth noticing, however, that in the treatise in which Plotinus records this acceptance[5] he goes beyond the Stoic

[1] VI. 9. 6; IV. 8. 7.

[2] VI. 9. I. Cp. S.V.F. II. 366; Sext. *Adv. Phys.* I. 78, and Witt, "Plotinus and Posidonius", *C.Q.* vol. XXIV, 1930, p. 203, and Reinhardt, *op. cit.* p. 45, etc.

[3] V. 7.

[4] Plut. *Comm. Not.* 36. 1077C; Sen. *Ep.* 113. 16; Marc. Aurel. 5. 3.

[5] V. 7.

position and argues vigorously against it. He is not opposing the Aristotelian doctrine that matter is the principle of individuation, which he barely mentions in the first chapter of the treatise. The arguments which he is concerned to rebut derive from the Stoic doctrines of the periodic return or restoration of all things, in which every individual entity and circumstance is reproduced with complete exactitude, and of the seminal logoi (in the form which asserted that the logos of the child was produced by a combination of the logoi of father and mother). His main anxiety, as stated at the beginning of the treatise, is the very un-Stoic one to ensure the status of the individual, of "Socrates himself" in the intelligible universe. His doctrine of the Ideas of individuals is primarily an aspect of his preoccupation with the individual soul. It must be admitted, however, that the Stoic doctrine of the ἰδίως ποιόν marks an important stage in the development from the primarily scientific preoccupations which led Aristotle to deny Forms of individuals to this concern of Plotinus for each man's soul by itself, not merely as an instance of the Form "man", just as the type of Stoic thought which is expressed in Marcus Aurelius's description of the soul which εἰς τὴν ἀπειρίαν τοῦ αἰῶνος ἐκτείνεται[1] marks a stage in the development from Aristotle's psychology to Plotinus's doctrine of "spiritual interpenetration".

We are, however, I think, justified in concluding that, in spite of several Stoic traits, Plotinus's world of Νοῦς is a unity-in-diversity in a Platonic or Aristotelian rather than a Stoic sense, not so much an organic body as a living system of Forms or a world in which Mind, minds and objects of intellection interpenetrate and are one. Thus the conceptions of Νοῦς as mind and Νοῦς as world are very closely bound up together. It is through Νοῦς as contemplating mind that the world of Forms is brought into relation with the One; and it is through its character as world of Forms contained in a mind which is its content that it is brought into contact with the visible universe. To this last Νοῦς is only archetype and source, by necessary generation, of the higher soul which governs and forms it. The higher world, with its self-contained life, neither exists for

[1] II. I.

the sake of the lower nor turns its attention towards it. In this lies the great difference between the Νοῦς of Plotinus and the Logos of Philo, which also contains the Forms;[1] Philo, being a fundamentally orthodox Jew, starts with God the Creator and the visible world his creature. The Logos, in so far as it can be said to have any separate existence at all,[2] is an instrument or intermediary used by God in creating the world; it exists, that is, or is postulated, for the sake of the visible world.[3] Such a conception is explicitly rejected by Plotinus[4] and would be a flat contradiction of the whole emphasis and direction of his system.

[1] *De Op. Mundi*, 24–5; *De Somn.* I. 62.
[2] Cp. Lebreton, *Histoire du Dogme de la Trinité*, vol. I, pp. 242–8.
[3] *De Cherub.* 125–7; *Leg. Alleg.* III. 96; *Q. Deus sit Immut.* 57, etc.
[4] VI. 7. 8.

Section III. SOUL

CHAPTER VI

SOUL, NATURE AND BODY

A STUDY of Plotinus's doctrine of the generation and governance of the visible world produces at first a rather bewildering impression. It is at this point that the enormous complexity of his philosophical inheritance becomes most manifest. The variations in his use of terms also make a good deal of difficulty. They are not, however, completely arbitrary, and a study of the words which Plotinus uses in different treatises for the formative and directing principles of the material universe is a useful help in following the variations of his thought.

The clash or tension in Plotinus's system between the two Platonic conceptions of this world as a prison for souls into which they fall by some pre-natal sin or inordinate desire and as a noble and necessary part of the universal order, an image of the Divine and itself a God, has often been dealt with. We must be careful not to misunderstand it. Plotinus always holds that the sense-world is good, and that its existence is a necessary completion of the universal order. Compared to the higher regions which it is possible for the human soul to inhabit it certainly appears less attractive, and may legitimately be described as a prison or a tomb, and the soul's descent to it as a fall. This status of the visible world in relation to the soul does not however affect its objective excellence. The visible world itself as a whole is not the product of a fallen or rebellious soul. The Gnostics' assertion that it was seemed to Plotinus a blasphemy. He does still feel the difficulty of combining this belief in the goodness of the sense-world with that in the fall of the soul, but tends to solve it by making the descent of individual souls happen in accordance with the universal law. All the same, there remains in his system a certain tension between the "world-accepting" and the "world-rejecting" temper. He is always faced with the problem of maintaining the absolute transcendence and self-sufficiency of the spiritual world, the true home of the soul, while at the same time making the existence of the material world rational and part of the order of things.

Plotinus's general view, at least up to the period of the very late treatises *On Providence*,[1] is that the world of the senses is informed and governed by Soul, which is conceived as having two activities, one immanent and one transcendent, the one giving existence, life, and form to material beings, the other directing the visible cosmos without being involved in it. I have already said something about the relation of this "higher Soul" to Νοῦς,[2] and have discussed the curious "spermatic" passages in which Plotinus seems to invert his system by making the material world an actualization of unrealized potentialities in the spiritual.[3] It remains to try to follow him through the elaborations of his account of the relation of the higher to the lower soul and of both to "body" or "matter". A good starting-point will be a passage in the first treatise of the Fifth Ennead.[4] Here we have the relation of Soul to Universe given in its simplest form. Soul is said to have made all living things, "breathing life into them...and itself (made) this great heaven, and itself adorned it, and itself conducts it round in order, being a nature (φύσις not here in its Plotinian technical sense) other than the things which it adorns and moves and makes live; and it is of necessity more honourable than these...". A little further on Plotinus speaks of the soul "which rushes and pours in from without (into the material universe) and enters it from every part and enlightens it". This is one of Plotinus's commonest thoughts, that soul is not in body but body in soul, that soul, itself remaining free and unbound by body (as far as the universal soul is concerned), enters the world of the senses and gives it form and life.[5]

At this point the complications begin. Soul, the Soul of the All, is thought of as the supreme directing, controlling, informing, everlastingly creative principle, working on the universe as something

[1] III. 2 and 3.
[2] Above, Ch. V.
[3] II. 9. 3; IV. 8. 6; V. 9. 6; above, Ch. IV.
[4] V. I. 2.
[5] Cp. IV. 3. 9; II. I. 3.

external to it. What, then, exactly does it work on? Simply matter? I do not think that Plotinus ever presents the cosmos as a bare duality of Soul and Matter. In the treatises *On Providence* he certainly shows the great Logos, the active power emanating from Soul, wrestling with matter and bringing it under form. There are plenty of passages where εἶδος or φύσις or λόγοι are coupled with ὕλη; but the transcendent Soul of the All does not act directly on ὕλη. The principle which does act directly on matter, when it is spoken of as a single principle, is a lower phase of Soul which becomes more and more clearly differentiated from the higher. Plotinus says,[1] "[the Soul] looking There, whence it came, is fertilized [or filled, πληροῦται], but going on to another and opposite movement generates an image of itself which is sensation and in plants [that is, organic living beings below the level of αἴσθησις] nature... it is not all present in plants, but it has come to be in plants because in advancing so far into the lower region it has made another hypostasis by its going forth and its eagerness for its inferior". Again in II. 1. 5, "the soul of the heaven is directly dependent on the Demiurge [here identified with Νοῦς] and so are ours; but an image (ἴνδαλμα) of it went forth and as it were flowed from the things that are above and made the living things on the earth"; and later in the same chapter: "We are formed by the soul which is given by the gods in the heavens and by the heavens themselves and are associated with bodies in virtue of it; for the other soul, according to which we are ourselves, is the cause of well-being, not of being." II. 3. 9 puts the conception especially clearly. "Everyone is double, one part the composite, one the Man Himself; and the whole universe is likewise double, one part being that compounded of body and a soul bound to body, and the other the Soul of the All which is not in body, but enlightens the traces [of itself] in that which is in body"; and again at the end of the chapter: "The universe is a god when That [the higher or separable soul] is reckoned with it, and the rest, Plato says, is a great daemon, and the affections in it are daemonic."[2]

[1] V. 2. 1.

[2] Both these last passages, of course, are commentaries on *Timaeus*, 41A ff. (the making of human beings by the Demiurge and the subordinate gods).

From these passages we can see that the Soul of the All organizes and governs not merely matter but a material world informed and ensouled by an emanation from itself. This emanation is to all intents and purposes a fourth hypostasis, a fourth stage in the descent of being from the One.[1] It is true that Plotinus denies this,[2] maintaining that there are three, and only three, Hypostases, and that no real division within them exists, and particularly emphasizing the unity of Soul. He is speaking there of the human soul, but the parallelism between it and the cosmic soul, between macrocosm and microcosm, is always very close in Plotinus. The passage, however, comes from the treatise *Against the Gnostics* and must be understood as a protest against their frenzied multiplication of aeons and emanations. In spite of it we cannot help seeing that the description in v. 2. 1 follows exactly the process by which one Plotinian hypostasis produces another. The perpetually recurring metaphor of the illumination of the lower by the higher also suggests this; and the division of Soul into θεός and δαίμων[3] makes it quite clear. We are justified in taking the lower soul as a distinct hypostasis and not simply as a "power" of the higher soul. Of course in Plotinus's system the distinction of hypostases is thought of as the mental recognition of real distinctions within a unity. The One interpenetrates all below it, and each of the lower hypostases derives its reality from submitting itself by contemplation as ὕλη to the higher from which it proceeds. The higher is the form, the principle of reality, to the lower, and so there is no very sharply defined frontier between the Beings. All I wish to make clear is that the "lower soul" really stands in much the same relation to the higher as Soul to Νοῦς.

What then are the nature and functions of this lower soul, and why did Plotinus find it necessary to his system? To understand the reason for its existence we must examine shortly the well-known contradiction in Plotinus's account of matter in the world of the senses. He varies between regarding it as a purely negative conception, absolute potency, and as a positively evil, anarchic force with a power of resisting form. The two ideas are often found

[1] Cp. ὑπόστασιν ἄλλην ποιησαμένη, v. 2. 1.
[2] II. 9. 2. [3] II. 3. 9.

combined, as in II. 4, where matter passes most curiously within the space of one treatise from Aristotelian potency to a positive evil. The second is found at its extremest in I. 8. We may perhaps say that the view of matter as potency is the one which Plotinus adopts when he is thinking as a pure metaphysician. The other is generally rather rhetorically expressed, and is closely bound up with his passionate conviction that man's soul can only find its true destiny in complete detachment from the material world; or sometimes it is introduced in passing as an easy explanation of evil, imperfection, and deformity in this world.[1] It is the old struggle of ideas that appears in Plato, which is explicitly discussed by Plotinus in IV. 8, between the intense desire for escape from the body in the *Phaedo* and the equally intense conviction of the goodness of the material world in the *Timaeus*.

The view of matter as pure potency is closely connected with the judgement that the material world is an excellent and necessary part of the universe, and is the one which is dominant in Plotinus's cosmology. This means that matter cannot in any way be responsible for the reality of the sense-world. This is certainly what Plotinus holds. For him all reality, in so far as it is real, is spiritual. There must, therefore, be an immanent spiritual principle in the world. It is difficult at first sight to see why this principle could not be the Soul of the All, which is concerned with the sensible world and acts as its guiding providence. This, combined with the equation of the Demiurge of the *Timaeus* with Νοῦς,[2] would have made his system closely parallel with Plato's cosmology and would also have provided a contact with the Stoic element in the tradition which he inherited. The transcendence of the spiritual would have been saved by the presence in the system of Νοῦς and the One.

The reasons why Plotinus does not adopt this exclusively immanentist view of the Universal Soul are to be found, I think, in the traditional account of Νοῦς which he inherited from Aristotle through the Middle Platonists and Neo-Pythagoreans and in his own psychological doctrine, which is firmly based on Plato. Νοῦς for Plotinus is not really the Demiurge. It is entirely turned in in

[1] II. 3. 11 and 16. [2] II. 1. 5.

self-contemplation and up to the contemplation of the One, not down to the world of the senses. It is far more closely related to the self-thinking Mind-God of Aristotle through the "higher mind" of Albinus and the First God of Numenius[1] than to anything in the *Timaeus*. Soul and the visible universe are unconscious by-products of its contemplation. This leaves the position of transcendent ruler and former of the visible world to be filled by the higher or universal Soul, and in view of Plato's teaching about the governance of the world by ψυχή and the change in the relation of ψυχή to Νοῦς that had taken place between Plato and Plotinus it was inevitable that for Plotinus it should be so filled. The necessity then arises of providing a hypostasis to take the place of the world-soul of the *Timaeus*, and this function is performed by the "lower soul".[2] This distribution of functions in the macrocosm is confirmed by the Platonic psychology of the microcosm in Plotinus. The two must obviously be closely related. Νοῦς and ψυχή in us are the universal Νοῦς and ψυχή. The universe is not cut off from the mind of man. The cardinal doctrine of Plato's psychology, as rightly understood by Plotinus, is that at least the highest part of soul is independent and detachable from the body, and rules the lusts and emotions as an incomer from a higher sphere in which it can be always present in contemplation. Plotinus's cosmic psychology is simply an application of Platonic individual psychology to the universe rather more systematic than anything in Plato, closely following the general outline of the *Timaeus* as far as concerns the lower hypostases,[3] but

[1] The detachment of Numenius's God, and its remoteness from all lower activities (see Ch. I, pp. 7–9 ff.) seem to me Aristotelian more than Oriental.

[2] In IV. 3. 2 Plotinus explicitly denies that the higher soul is the "soul of the cosmos". It is αὐτὴ ἐφ' ἑαυτῆς, not "of" anything (a very common way of expressing transcendence in the *Enneads*). It is not however clear that the soul of the cosmos in this passage, a "partial" soul in virtue of its specific function, like the souls of individuals, is to be identified with the "lower soul" of other passages, cp. Ch. 6.

[3] Plato of course does not give any clear or systematic description of the relation between the Demiurge and the World-Soul in the *Timaeus*; cp. Cornford, *Plato's Cosmology*, pp. 38–9. Here as always in comparing the *Timaeus* with the *Enneads* we must remember that the one is a myth, the other a collection of expositions of a system.

with the addition of a transcendent self-contemplating Νοῦς containing and informed by Plato's world of Forms.

The belief in the independence of Soul, its transcendence of the world of the senses, is possibly affected by the conception of matter as a source of evil, which it would be a contamination to the higher soul to touch too closely. The connection between the two ideas is not however really very close. Plotinus certainly seems to think of the descent of the individual soul towards matter as, not exactly a sin, but a falling below the highest. One feels that in the society of Souls a descent into the world of the senses must have been regarded rather as some people in nineteenth-century England regarded a visit to the W.C., a necessary compliance with a regrettable and unmentionable law of nature. To descend deeper than necessary into matter is for Plotinus a sin, but it is a sin rather of self-isolation than of self-pollution.[1] The idea of self-pollution does also occur, but it has not the same philosophical importance for Plotinus as the idea of self-isolation, which belongs to the scheme of ever-increasing multiplicity proceeding from unity which is an essential part of his thought. In the One there is unity without diversity, in Νοῦς complete unity-in-diversity, every part is the whole, and the whole in every part. The same is true of the individual souls in Soul.[2] The unity of thought and object of thought is, however, less complete in Soul. It has the faculty of discursive reason, no longer of intuitive;[3] all the objects of thought are not simultaneously and eternally present in it. The material world is a stage of still greater separateness. The spatial property of the mutual exclusiveness of substances belongs to it. Hence in proportion as soul gives itself more and more to the material world it becomes more and more isolated. The universal soul is universal, is not bound up with any partial entity simply because it is universal in its outlook, not preoccupied like individual souls with its individual interests; hence it stands in the closest relation to the universal Νοῦς.[4] It is all the same perfectly

[1] Cp. IV. 8. 4: μεταβάλλουσαι δὲ ἐκ τοῦ ὅλου εἰς τὸ μέρος τε εἶναι καὶ ἑαυτῶν καὶ οἷον κάμνουσαι τῷ σὺν ἄλλῳ εἶναι ἀναχωροῦσιν εἰς τὸ αὑτῶν ἑκάστη; VI. 4. 16.

[2] IV. 3. 8; V. 1. 2; VI. 4. 14. [3] V. 1. 3–4. [4] IV. 3. 6.

possible for the soul in the material world to be fully united with the higher spheres. The "flight" of the soul is for Plotinus a turning to the higher while still in the body. Even the mystical union with the One is within the reach of the embodied soul. There is no suggestion in the *Enneads* that the souls of the stars are hampered by their material bodies, though these bodies are formed of fire and not of any mysterious quintessence.[1] The only thing that can hamper the soul is its own sin of self-centredness, which proceeds from within itself and is not due to admixture with matter. There is, I think, no passage in the *Enneads* where Soul or souls are said to be spoilt or thwarted by ὕλη. λόγος and εἶδος are said to be thwarted by ὕλη[2] and λόγοι to be corrupted by it.[3] This goes to confirm the complete Platonism of Plotinus's account of soul. It is in body, but independent of it and transcending it in its highest activity, never simply its form or actuality, and so not liable to be affected by it. This Platonic conception of soul leaves the reality of the sense-world and its amenability to the providential directions of soul unaccounted for. For this reason Plotinus introduces the lower soul sharply separated from the higher.[4]

The individual, and particularly the human, soul seems for Plotinus to occupy an intermediate place between the lower and higher, or rather to contain both lower and higher in it. It is distinguished from the universal soul by its concern for the particular body with which it is bound up, by its absorption in its specialized individual task.[5] This specialization, though from one point of view, already considered, it can be thought of as a sin or defect, from another point of view is the result of a necessary law of the universal order, and is a means whereby the sensible is brought as fully as possible into contact with the intelligible.[6] The individual souls are a vital part of the cosmic order because both lower and higher worlds are multiple and diverse as well as unified. Each soul, that is, stands in the same relation to a particular Νοῦς-νοητόν in the

[1] II. 2. 3, etc. [2] II. 3. 11. [3] I. 8. 8.

[4] Cp. II. 1. 5, where we are said to have two souls, one the cause of our being, the other of our well-being, and VI. 7. 5.

[5] IV. 3. 12–18. [6] IV. 3. 12–13, 8. 7.

intelligible world as the universal soul to the universal Νοῦς.[1] Further, the individual soul "does not altogether come down".[2] It remains in part always in the higher realm of universality and, as we have seen, if it realizes its true nature can take upon itself its natural, eternal universality and "become the All" even in the body.[3] Individual souls never simply exist in and for the material world, are not completely bound up in it, though they are not as completely detached from the material world as is the higher or universal soul. Their relations with the lower soul or "nature" and with body will perhaps become clearer after a more detailed examination of the way in which Plotinus conceives of this φύσις as working in the world of the senses.

The most obvious element in Plotinus's doctrine of the "lower soul" is that suggested by the name which he most often gives it, φύσις. His conception of this "nature" has a good deal in common with Aristotle's, but it is not as completely Aristotelian as his choice of name would imply. It would be an undue simplification, though one not altogether remote from the truth, to say that Plotinus's account of the material world is an elaboration of that of Aristotle, just as his account of the world of spirit is an elaboration of that of Plato. Some points in his terminology would support this view. In one passage, for instance, he contrasts rather strikingly the εἴδη τῶν σωμάτων with the λόγοι περὶ ψυχήν,[4] using the Aristotelian word for the forms immanent in bodies. But, passing over minor differences, for example the rejection of a fifth element for the heavenly bodies, the comparison breaks down just where at first sight it looks as if it would be clearest, in the account of "nature". Plotinus's belief in the goodness and value of the material world which might be regarded as a link with Aristotle really of course derives from the later writings of Plato. It is the point of view of an imaginative and religious Platonist rather than that of a great biologist determined to subdue and correct his persistent Platonism to comply with the postulates of natural science and scientific thinking.

[1] IV. 3. 14. [2] IV. 8. 8; IV. 3. 12, 15.

[3] Cp. however IV. 3. 17. The needs of the body can and must interfere at times with the higher life of individual souls. [4] II. 4. 12.

The passages in the *Enneads* which I take as showing Aristotle's influence are those which represent nature as an unconscious immanent life-force. (There is also one passage[1] where it is described in terms strongly suggesting the active desiring ὕλη of *Physics*, I.[2]) They certainly belong to the Platonic-Aristotelian tradition and have little in common with the Stoic doctrine of an immanent material vital principle. Nature in Plotinus is always immaterial, always belongs to the class of soul. Further, he speaks of it as an "image" or "impression" of the higher soul[3] and of the higher soul as irradiating it.[4] That is, it has its due place in the scheme of informed emanation, in which the universe is thought of as composed of differing levels of being, clearly separated from each other, of which each is given reality by that immediately above it. The Stoic element in Plotinus's account of the sense-world is to be found in his conception of it as an organic whole,[5] which to some extent conflicts with the conception of levels of being. The most common sign of Stoic influence in Plotinus's account of the relations of the soul and the sense-world is to be found in his frequent mention of the spermatic, immanent, forming Logoi,[6] which he mentions without explanation as using a conception generally understood. The likeness of his Logoi in matter to the Spermatic Logoi of the Stoics is, however, diminished by the fact that he always thinks of them as images or emanations of the individual souls or soul-Logoi,[7] and these in their turn of the Logoi in Νοῦς.[8] He speaks often of the "unfolding" of the Logoi from higher to lower. In fact, though Plotinus takes over the conception of the Logoi in matter as living forms or forming-forces from Stoicism he as always adapts them most radically to the needs and conceptions of his own system. In the treatise *On the Problems of the Soul* in the Fourth Ennead and still more noticeably in VI. 7. 5 the immanent Logoi are rather Aristotelian dependents of Platonic transcendent souls than like anything in Stoic doctrine. Nature, too, for Plotinus is not a Logos

[1] II. 4. 3.
[2] 192a.
[3] IV. 4. 13.
[4] II. 3. 9.
[5] See next Chapter.
[6] IV. 3. 8, 10, 4. 11.
[7] IV. 3. 11; VI. 7. 5; cp. VI. 7. 9.
[8] IV. 3. 5.

Spermatikos and does not contain Logoi Spermatikoi. The Logoi which it contains are clearly distinguished from the Logoi in bodies[1] and it is not immanent in the same way. Stoic influence on Plotinus's thought usually shows itself rather in the words he uses and in points of detail than in the broad outlines of his system.

Three passages from the Second, Third and Fourth Enneads will serve as a convenient text for a more precise discussion of the relation of Plotinus's conception of "nature" to that of Aristotle. It will be convenient to deal with the latter two first. Here we find Plotinus starting from the conception of "nature" as a force which is unthinking but yet does its work in the world in a rational and ordered manner.[2] He says that nature "does not know, but only acts"[3] and in the eighth treatise of the Third Ennead poses the problem of "how nature, which they say is without the image-making faculty and irrational, has contemplation in itself and makes what it makes through contemplation which it does not possess".[4] It is in Plotinus's solution of this problem[5] that the difference between his thought and Aristotle's appears most clearly. While it is true that for him the visible universe is produced by a process of "necessary emanation" without reasoning or forethought[6] its production is an unconscious reflex of a contemplation, the strange, dream-like contemplation of nature.[7] It has passed over from the world of thought to that of sense because of the weakness of nature's contemplation as compared with that of the higher soul. The teaching of the whole of this strange and fascinating treatise *On Contemplation* is that contemplation is the proper activity of anything that can be brought into the category of "soul" in the widest sense, nature, life, or Logos. Nature, like the higher hypostases, has this primary activity, turned inwards upon itself. The giving of life and reality to the beings of the sense-world is a secondary activity, a by-product, both for nature and for individual souls, either unconscious or the result of a failure in contemplation.

[1] IV. 3. II.

[2] Cp. Ross, *Aristotle*, pp. 185–6, for this notion of "unconscious teleology" in Aristotle.

[3] IV. 4. 13.

[4] III. 8. I.

[5] III. 8. 2–4.

[6] III. 2. I.

[7] III. 8. 4.

Action is presented, that is, as an incidental consequence of or an inferior substitute for contemplation. For Aristotle, on the other hand, nature is essentially the principle of movement in the sensible world. Contemplation does not occur till we reach the human soul at its highest. In the lower reaches of soul activity in the material world is primary, not, as for Plotinus, secondary and incidental. Even the lowest soul for Plotinus is not Aristotelian because it is not truly or solely immanent. This conclusion is confirmed by the passage from the Second Ennead[1] where the lower soul is said to be bound not to matter but to body. Body in Plotinus always means the concretum of matter and the dead, lowest form, with a sort of shadow of soul and life in it. Plotinus is here again consistent in his acceptance of Plato's doctrine of the independence of soul and his rejection of Aristotle's that the soul is the form of the body. Nature is only immanent in a sense compatible with transcendence. It is not truly united with matter to form the single living creature as it is in Aristotle.[2]

Plotinus's conception of the relation of nature to body is most clearly stated in the second treatise *On the Problems of the Soul.* Here he says:[3] "The shape which it [Nature] gives to that which is formed is to be taken as another form distinct from nature itself."[4] This quite clearly distinguishes nature from what it makes, and makes it clear that its production and not itself is the immanent form in body. The nature of body is made clear by passages in Chs. 18 and 20. In Ch. 18 "the body of animals and plants" is said to have as it were a shadow of soul and to be the subject of pain and bodily pleasure. In Ch. 20 it is said: "Nor can the origin of appetite and purpose be put down to undetermined body, nor the quest of bitter or sweet to the soul itself, but [all this must belong to] what is body, but wishes to be not only body but has acquired a greater variety of movements than soul and has been compelled by its acquisition to aim at a great number of objects." Plotinus goes on to deal with the question of desire and states definitely that there are two ἐπιθυμίαι, one in body and one in nature. He describes nature

[1] II. 3. 9.
[2] Cp. VI. 7. 6.
[3] Ch. 14.
[4] Cp. IV. 3. 11; III. 2. 17, 8. 2.

as intermediate between body and perception. The function of the latter is to pass on the image resulting from the desire of nature, the conscious formulation of the desire, to the higher soul, which is alone responsible for deciding whether the desire is to be satisfied or not.[1] In his explanation of why there are two ἐπιθυμίαι, Plotinus says: "Nature is one thing, and the body which becomes determinate (τὸ τοιόνδε) through nature another; for nature exists before the coming into being of the determinate body. It itself makes the determinate body, moulding and shaping it. If this is so, it cannot be the origin of desire but [it must start with] the determinate body...but nature is like a mother guessing at the wishes of the suffering body and trying to set it right and lead it back to herself; and in searching for the remedy it attaches itself to the desire of the sufferer and the determination of the desire is transmitted from the body to nature (καὶ τὴν περάτωσιν ἀπ' ἐκείνου πρὸς αὐτὴν ἥκειν); so that one might say that desire originated from the determinate body, but nature desires as a result of and because of something other than itself. The granting or withholding of the desire is other again [and belongs to the higher soul]."

The most noticeable points of this are, first the complete separation of nature and at the same time its complete preoccupation with the affairs of body and, second, the use of τὸ τοιόνδε σῶμα instead of simply σῶμα. This, with the words πλάττουσα καὶ μορφοῦσα,[2] shows that the desiring body of this passage is certainly informed, is a compound of form and matter. The distinction between nature in Plotinus and nature in Aristotle is therefore quite clear. The description of body and its desires does, however, bring Plotinus's account of the sense-world close to Aristotle's. Even here, however, there is a radical difference. Form and matter never really for Plotinus unite into an organic whole. Matter remains unchanged by the forms externally superimposed upon it.[3] It is always darkness, negation, falsehood, a phantasm of reality. Here more than anywhere else in the system the idea of organic unity gives place to that of sharply separate levels of being.

[1] Cp. Ch. 28. [2] Cp. τῷ πλασθέντι in Ch. 14.
[3] II. 4. 16, 5. 5.

The driving force in Plotinus's σῶμα seems to have two functions. It desires to be "not only body" and consequently possesses movement; and it is the primary principle of desire. This is very suggestive of the drive towards actualization in Aristotle's material world and the function of nature as an immanent "principle of motion and rest". There is a passage in Ch. 27 of this same treatise which is worth quoting in this connection. It runs: "We must consider that every part has a trace [of the principle of growth] and on this is superimposed the universal principle of growth, which does not belong to particular things but to the whole. Then comes the perceptive nature, no longer mingled with body, but resting upon it (ἐποχουμένη); then the other soul and Νοῦς." Here, as in Ch. 20, we have both the principle of growth, or nature strictly so-called, and the principle of perception, intervening between individual things of sense, informed bodies, and the "other" or higher soul. Nature seems to be more fully immanent, more "mingled with body", than perception, to which the word ἐποχουμένη (which seems to mean in Plotinus "transcending, but in contact") is applied. The clearest distinction between it and the "traces" of soul in the parts is that it is not of any particular part but of the whole. If we take this with Plotinus's other teaching about the relation of whole and part[1] and about the sharp separation between nature and body we can see that nature is not simply the mechanical sum of its parts in individual things. The whole in Plotinus is never a mere aggregate of parts except in material things, and nature is not material, and cannot, like individual human souls, "fall" into the separateness of the material world. It is the lowest part of the *universal* soul. This makes the function of nature in the universe more intelligible. It is the principle of unity and wholeness which prevents the material world from falling apart into anarchy, and it is this because it is the one life and life-giver. This makes the meaning of its separateness easier to understand. It can be said to be bound to body or mingled with body because it is wholly concerned with body. The material world is its reason for existing and it is

[1] This is clearly shown in what he says about Soul and individual souls in the early part of IV. 3.

part in a sense of the structure of that world. It is the part of soul which has the function of giving life and reality to body by making it determinate. It remains, however, soul as Plato conceived it, not a form or principle of reality inseparable from matter. It is the last stage but one in the evolution of the Many from the primal Unity. It provides that unity underlying the extreme multiplicity of the material world without which it could not exist.

The position of αἴσθησις in these passages is noticeable. There is not, I think, enough evidence for thinking that Plotinus ever regarded it as a separate hypostasis intervening between the higher soul and nature. Its intermediate position and apparent separateness, however, do show his tendency to an ever greater multiplication and subdivision of the levels of being. This is particularly evident in the region between the higher soul and matter, where Plotinus is at the same time trying to vindicate the independence and transcendence of soul and to provide an unbroken connection reaching down to the lowest level of reality. This was made easy for him by the theories of emanation and of the counter-movement by which the lower returns upon the higher and is informed by it. The fantastically elaborate systems of later Neo-Platonism show the disastrous consequences of this way of thinking.

Nature in these passages, even when consciousness or contemplation is attributed to it, is not a regulative force. In IV. 4. 20 the decision whether a desire is to be yielded to or resisted lies with soul, not with nature. Nature is simply a forming and hence life-giving principle.

Chapter VII

THE MATERIAL UNIVERSE AS AN ORGANIC WHOLE. THE GREAT LOGOS

The sense-world for Plotinus, though it represents the lowest and extremest degree of multiplicity, is not simply an anarchy. It is an organic whole. We have already seen that the lower soul is a unifying principle, and this unification of the material universe by soul is a doctrine of great importance to Plotinus. It is expounded most fully in the last chapters of the second treatise *On the Problems of the Soul* and in the early chapters of VI. 7 and in a different form in the treatises of the Third Ennead *On Providence*. There is no formal change of doctrine in these chapters, but there is a certain difference of emphasis. The distinctions between higher and lower soul and between lower soul and that vestige of soul which is the form of body are maintained throughout the treatises in which the unity of the organic universe is stressed.[1]

Plotinus has three ways of approaching the problem of fitting the organic visible universe into his system. The first, as Bréhier says, follows the *Timaeus* closely, but with many Stoic touches. It is set forth in those chapters of the second treatise *On the Problems of the Soul* where Plotinus is discussing the consciousness of the star-gods and the way in which magical incantations operate. These were questions of extreme importance to his age, dominated as it was by magic, astrology, and astral religion, and it is not surprising that in answering them he should approach more closely than usual to the common beliefs of his time. The firm Platonic foundation of the belief in the "visible living creature"[2] would enable him to do so

[1] VI. 7. 4, 5 and 6, especially Ch. 6: ἐλλάμπει δ' οὗτος τῷ δευτέρῳ καὶ οὗτος τῷ τρίτῳ· ἔχει δέ πως πάντας ὁ ἔσχατος οὐ γινόμενος ἐκείνοις, ἀλλὰ παρακείμενος ἐκείνοις; III. 2. 2, 3. 4.

[2] *Timaeus*, 92 C.

with a clear conscience. His solution is that all the parts of the visible universe, including men and the star-divinities, are enabled to act reciprocally upon each other because they are parts of the one living All, and hence bound together by a universal sympathy.[1] Not only can the parts affect each other but their reciprocal action is determined by the All, which moves them as a dancer moves his limbs, not consciously directing each movement but with his mind fixed on the performance as a whole, the various motions following automatically and unconsciously[2] (a superb example of the subtlety and accuracy of Plotinus's metaphors). This movement is not like that of an external cause acting on something other than itself; ἀλλ' αὐτὸν πάντα τὰ γινόμενα εἶναι.[3] There is no inconsistency in this with Plotinus's usual doctrine. The soul of the All, though separate and transcendent, is never in Plotinus "outside" the visible universe. It is intimately present to it, whole to whole and part to part. The distinctions, too, within soul between lower, higher, and partial are maintained by the doctrine, put forward at the beginning of Ch. 32, that the parts participate in the body of the All equally, in its soul in varying degrees and according as they participate or not in any "other" (presumably partial) soul. The degree to which the immanence of soul, its close connection with body, is emphasized is, however, rather unusual in Plotinus. Theiler is quite probably right in seeing in these chapters traces of the influence of Posidonius;[4] as long as this is not taken to imply that Plotinus's thought ever had anything really in common with the crude immanentism of the Stoics. Even when Plotinus asserts with the greatest emphasis the continuity of all reality and its unbroken evolution from its source, and the penetration of soul even into the darkness of matter, to the lowest limit of being,[5] he always maintains the division of reality into clearly distinguishable levels.

[1] Ch. 32. [2] Ch. 33.

[3] On this doctrine Plotinus bases an entirely magical account of prayer, Chs. 40–42; there is no question of any act of will on the part of the divinities addressed; the answer comes automatically and unconsciously through the working of the universal organism.

[4] *Vorbereitung des Neu-Platonismus*, Ch. 2.

[5] As in IV. 8. 6; II. 9. 3.

His evolutionary or rather emanationist doctrine has not very much in common with Stoic theories of the evolution of individual or universe from a "seed" or Spermatic Logos. The "unfolding of the Logoi" in the *Enneads* is not a real process of evolution. It is the necessary and undeliberate actualization of the potentialities which the higher contains for producing the lower, and results from the capacity in the higher for contemplating that above itself again.[1] The material world is "dead", a "corpse adorned" because unproductive, and unproductive because in it the last vestige of soul has fallen below the capacity for contemplation.[2]

The second way in which Plotinus deals with his problem is closely related to the first. It is to be found in the early chapters of the treatise *On the Multiplicity of the Forms and on the Good.* Here the wholeness and organic character of the visible universe is assumed. It is simply stated in Ch. 2. Plotinus's attention is concentrated on the intelligible universe. The wholeness and perfection of the visible universe, the existence and disposition of each of the parts so as to complete the whole, depend not on any conscious planning but on the existence of that higher All, the unity-in-diversity of Νοῦς. The transcendence of the higher soul, and in particular of the higher human soul, is stressed[3] rather than its immanent ensouling of the material universe. The universal transcendent soul and its individual souls are here conceived after the manner of the *Timaeus* as the intermediaries by which the sense-world is formed on the model of the intelligible. In this connection we find a rather complex treatment of the relation of individual souls to the universal soul. The universal soul makes a preparatory sketch (προϋπογραφή) of the pattern of the visible universe which is, as it were, a "preliminary illumination" of matter. According to this pattern the individual souls have to work, and it depends upon it whether they have the opportunity to produce and ensoul the higher (man) or must content themselves with the lower animals.[4] The process of making the preparatory sketch perhaps corresponds to the production of determinate body by nature, which is the lowest

[1] III. 8.
[2] III. 8. 2.
[3] Chs. 4 and 5.
[4] Ch. 7; cp. IV. 3. 6.

phase of universal soul, in the passages already quoted. The individual souls are compared to craftsmen who can only make ὃ ἡ ὕλη ἐθέλει τῇ ἐπιτηδειότητι, which suggests that what they are really dealing with is not ὕλη in the strict sense, pure potency, but informed matter, σῶμα, or determinate body.

This description seems to reduce the power of choice of the individual soul to a minimum. It is therefore rather surprising to find in the preceding chapter that blame attaches to the soul for producing anything lower than man. καθαρὰ μὲν οὖν οὖσα καὶ πρὶν κακυνθῆναι ἄνθρωπον θέλει καὶ ἄνθρωπος ἔστι. It is the old difficulty, of which Plotinus is fully conscious, which arises whenever he tries to reconcile the moral responsibility of the individual soul for its own destiny with the universal all-embracing order. It is intensified here, however, by the prominence given to the intelligible universe as archetype of the sensible. The archetypes of everything in this world, men, animals, plants, the earth itself, are present There as living forms, sharing in the eternal glory of the intelligible universe.[1] If this is so, it is difficult to see how attraction to one of them more than another should be a sign of degradation in the soul. They are all noble and necessary parts of the Divine All, pig or beetle or toadstool as well as man, and their production in the lower world is necessary to the perfection of the visible All, itself noble and divine. There does seem to be a conflict here, real though not fully expressed, between the concept of the sensible world as a whole single and unified, an organism and a copy as a whole of a higher organism, and the concept of it as a ladder leading down through successive steps of degeneration from the light of soul to the darkness of matter. It must be remembered, however, that for Plotinus man is a "bridge-being", intermediate between the two worlds. He alone is present in the intelligible personally in his own right, the other creatures only by their archetypes. It is therefore in a way natural that Plotinus should make the "man of this world" the lowest point to which the soul can descend without sin. This does not, however, entirely remove the contradiction.

In spite of the presence of this doctrine of man as a "bridge-being",

[1] Chs. 9–12.

which seems to have played an important part in the thought of Posidonius,[1] I cannot altogether accept Theiler's view that these chapters, like those of IV. 4 which I have just discussed, are deeply influenced by Posidonius. The reason for this I have given at length in an earlier chapter.[2] It is, in short, that the account of the unity-in-diversity of the intelligible universe given here is fundamentally un-Stoic, and has clearly recognizable sources in the thought of Plato and Aristotle. The most that we can say in favour of an influence of later Stoicism here is that it is possible to regard the world of Νοῦς as a hypostatization of the Stoic concept of an eternal world-order. This is not, however, the origin of Plotinus's conception, as I have tried to show.

The third form which the doctrine of the organic visible universe takes in Plotinus is to be found in the treatises *On Providence*.[3] It stands rather apart from the other two, and is marked by a still greater stressing of the transcendence of soul. The treatises are a work of Plotinus's last period, and show a remarkable development of his thought. Their most striking feature is the appearance in them of the doctrine of the Logos. This is the most extreme modification which the doctrine of the three hypostases ever undergoes in the *Enneads*. The Logos is a fourth hypostasis even more clearly than nature, and a hypostasis, moreover, whose own structure is complex. It is introduced[4] in the words Νοῦς τοίνυν δούς τι ἑαυτοῦ εἰς ὕλην ἀτρεμὴς καὶ ἥσυχος τὰ πάντα εἰργάζετο· τοῦτο δὲ λόγος ἐκ νοῦ ῥυείς. τὸ γὰρ ἀπορρέον ἐκ νοῦ λόγος, καὶ ἀεὶ ἀπορρεῖ, ἕως ἂν ᾖ παρὼν ἐν τοῖς οὖσι νοῦς. From this it would seem that the Logos takes the place of Soul as an intermediary between Νοῦς and the visible world. It is the emanation from Νοῦς through which its potentiality of producing that below it is actualized without movement or effort in the higher, according to the familiar Plotinian doctrine. It is the means by which Νοῦς is present in the visible world. Another passage[5] makes it clear that Plotinus did not mean

[1] Theiler, *l.c.*; Jaeger, *Nemesios von Emesa*; Witt, "Plotinus and Posidonius", *C.Q.* vol. XXIV, 1930, p. 198.

[2] Ch. V.

[3] III. 2 and 3.

[4] III. 2. 2.

[5] Ch. 16.

to exclude Soul from the series of Hypostases. Here he says: ἔστι τοίνυν οὗτος ὁ λόγος...οὐκ ἄκρατος νοῦς οὐδ' αὐτόνους οὐδέ γε ψυχῆς καθαρᾶς τὸ γένος, ἠρτημένος δὲ ἐκείνης καὶ οἷον ἔκλαμψις ἐξ ἀμφοῖν, νοῦ καὶ ψυχῆς κατὰ νοῦν διακειμένης γεννησάντων τὸν λόγον τοῦτον, ζωὴν λόγον τινὰ ἡσυχῇ ἔχουσαν.[1] Even here, though Soul has its part in the generation of the Logos it is noteworthy that Plotinus still brings it into very close connection with Νοῦς, to which it is not said to be related indirectly or through the intermediary of Soul. It is an "outshining from both". Soul produces it because it is "disposed in accordance with Νοῦς". The treatises *On Providence* form a theodicy, a justification of the moral order in our world. The Logos, as the cause of this order, is the representative of Νοῦς, of the transcendent divine order because of which this world is an ordered whole. It discharges the functions in the sense-world attributed in earlier treatises to the Universal Soul. The individual souls are its parts[2] and also seem to be Logoi of higher souls in the Universal Soul, now completely withdrawn from this world.[3] The Logos is a unifying principle, the harmonizer.[4] It stands itself midway in point of unity between the higher world of Νοῦς and Soul and the sense-world which it produces. Its function is to produce in that world the best sort of unity of which it is capable, a Heraclitean παλίντονος ἁρμονίη, the unity of a well-constructed play dealing with strife and battles.[5] All this corresponds closely to the account of the government of the sense-world by the Universal Soul given in the treatises *Against the Gnostics* and *On the Problems of the Soul*.[6] The ethical tone, too, in the description of the rule of the Logos is very similar to that of the earlier passages. There is the same passionate vindication of the goodness and justice of the order of the visible universe, and the same austere insistence that the suffering or degradation, even the sin, of individuals contributes to the good of the whole, expressed in the simile of the tortoise and the dance (compare the great picture of the Dancer in the second treatise *On the Problems of the Soul*).

[1] Cp. 3. 3. [2] 2. 17, 18.
[3] 3. 1. [4] 2. 2, 3. 1.
[5] 2. 16, 17. [6] II. 9. 7; IV. 4. 3.

The Logos is represented in the treatises *On Providence* as the one intermediary between the higher and lower worlds. There is nothing below it but the sense-world which it produces. It thus combines the functions of the two universal soul-hypostases of the earlier treatises, the higher soul and nature. The Logos is in direct contact with matter.[1] The division between the higher and lower phases of Universal Soul is represented by a division between a higher and lower Logos or Pronoia,[2] which is brought into close connection with the common Plotinian doctrine of the multiplicity of "men", the higher and lower principles in the human soul.[3] In another passage[4] we have this duality of higher and lower expressed rather differently, as a duality of Pronoia and Heimarmene. In the very early treatise III. 1[5] Heimarmene appears as the limitation imposed on soul in body by its environment in the material world. This conception is developed in particular in the concluding chapters of IV. 4 which deal with the universal sympathy, the all-controlling law of the sense-world. The two chapters[6] which explain the degree to which the sage, the true philosopher, is free from the operation of this law stand particularly close to the earlier discussion. We shall probably be justified in taking the Heimarmene of the passage in III. 3, which is described as ἀπὸ τοῦ χείρονος ἀρξαμένη, but is a part of the one Pronoia, as being the all-embracing law of universal sympathy or harmony in the material universe, the law on which such efficacy as magic or astrology possesses depends. It is the Logos working in the sense-world and imposing on it that kind of order which is suited to it.[7]

1 3. 4.
2 3. 4.
3 Cp. VI. 7. 6.
4 3. 5.
5 Chs. 8, 9.
6 IV. 4. 43–44.

7 The distinction made between the higher Pronoia and the lower Heimarmene marks the divergence between the Stoic and the Middle Platonist teaching on the subject of the latter. For the Stoics Pronoia and Heimarmene were the same, cp. S.V.F. II. 913 (Chrysippus). In his distinction between grades of Pronoia and his placing the higher above Heimarmene Plotinus follows the Middle Platonist tradition represented by Ps.-Plutarch, *De Fato* (cp. especially Ps.-Plut. 9 ff., also Nemesius, *d. Nat. Hom.* 44, Albinus, *Didaskalikos* 14, Chalcidius, *Comm. in Platonis Timaeum* 150 ff. (pp. 207 ff. Wrobel)).

The Logos in these treatises appears to have taken over all the functions of the Universal Soul in relation to the sense-world. The account of the generation of the Logos from Νοῦς and soul, as well as of the individual souls in the Logos from the parts of the transcendent soul, suggests that there is a real distinction between the two hypostases. M. Bréhier, in his introduction to the treatises,[1] suggests that the two are rather to be considered as two aspects of the same thing. This is supported by the fact that for Plotinus soul and nature are always Logoi[2] and by the appearance in Ch. 2 of the first treatise *On Providence* of soul in its usual place of ruler of the sense-world, which is occupied throughout the rest of the treatises by the Logos. The balance of evidence, however, seems to be in favour of regarding Soul and the Logos as distinct. Soul has withdrawn entirely to the higher world, to the realm of Νοῦς, there presumably to engage in its primary activity of contemplation. Its secondary activity of generating and governing the sense-world has been taken over by the Logos. The two, of course, though distinct, are not for Plotinus separate. The Logos is of the nature of soul. They are, however, to be distinguished as clearly as soul and nature in the earlier treatises, though the Logos cannot, as we have seen, be correlated with nature or the lower soul. It discharges the functions in the sense-world of both higher and lower. It is a regulative as well as a unifying force.

The account given in the treatises *On Providence* of Soul and the Logos is the furthest Plotinus ever went in stressing the transcendence of the generative and governing principle of the material universe. It has something in common with the spirit of the contemporary treatise *On the Knowing Hypostases*.[3] Here we find a sharp separation of the different levels of being and an exceptionally strong assertion of the incompatibility of the lower soul with the spiritual life in the realm of Νοῦς. "[The knowledge of the most divine part of soul as a means to the knowledge of Νοῦς] is only possible if you cut away first the body from the man—that is from yourself—and then the soul which forms the body, and then most

[1] Budé ed. III, pp. 17–23.
[2] III. 8. 2, 6; VI. 7. 7.
[3] V. 3.

certainly perception and desires and emotions and all such fooleries, which incline strongly towards the mortal."[1] In this sharply other-worldly asceticism we have the correlative for the spiritual life of this latest phase of Plotinus's cosmology. It is interesting to see that there is little trace in the treatises *On Providence* of the extreme dualism of another almost contemporary treatise, I. 8 *On Evil*, the locus classicus in the *Enneads* for the conception of matter as the principle of evil. There is a casual allusion in III. 2. 2 to the 'Ανάγκη of the *Timaeus* as an irrational principle hampering the work of reason in the world, but it is not developed further. The dominant conception in the treatises is that of the universal organic order, finely expressed in 2. 3 (the speech of the Universe). Plotinus carries this conception so far as to say that the Logos (universal or individual) contains within itself the Logos of its matter ἣν αὐτῷ ἐργάσεται ποιώσας καθ' αὑτὸν τὴν ὕλην ἢ σύμφωνον εὑρών.[2] The context (the form or Logos always fitted to its appropriate matter), however, suggests that it is informed matter that is in question and the conception is the same as that of the "preparatory outline" of IV. 4 and VI. 7. But there is certainly no dualism in the treatises of the kind which makes matter the principle of evil. It would perhaps be true to say that Plotinus only holds this view when he is considering matter in isolation. When he is looking at the material world as a whole, from the point of view of soul, he regards it as an ensouled organic unity, good and necessary as a whole and in every part.

The immediate historical background of these treatises is Stoic. Their ethical thought in particular is in the Stoic tradition, and many detailed parallels can be drawn.[3] Their Heracliteanism, both in its ethical and cosmological aspects, brings them into close contact with the later, "Posidonian", Stoicism.[4] The austerity of Plotinus's application of Heraclitean principles to the problem of suffering is in the Stoic tradition of Marcus Aurelius and Epictetus. The rather depressingly complacent optimism which sometimes appears in earlier Stoic views of the world-order[5] is no longer

[1] Ch. 9; cp. Ch. 17: Ἄφελε πάντα.
[2] 3. 4.
[3] Cp. Bréhier's Introduction to the treatises, Budé ed. III, pp. 17–23.
[4] Cp. *De Mundo*, 5.
[5] Cp. Bréhier, *Chrysippe*, p. 143.

apparent in the Stoics of the post-Christian centuries. The "Stoic" scale of unity, too, appears in Chs. 16 and 17; though, as we have seen, Plotinus whenever he uses it gives it a thoroughly un-Stoic turn and makes it serve the ends of his own very different doctrine of the hierarchy of unity. The transcendent Logos, on the other hand, is a thoroughly un-Stoic conception. To some extent we can find an origin for it in Plotinus's own thought. These treatises are primarily a vindication of the belief in a moral order and government of the world. Plotinus may well, therefore, have felt the need to present the Divine power working in the world as simply as possible, as a single principle emanating from the higher Divine order. Logos for him is a generic term for the principle of reality and order, the forming force, whether individual or universal, in every level of being. Thus it would be natural enough for him to make the principle of order in the sense-world a universal Logos, particularly in a controversial treatise directed against those who would deny such an order.

If we are to look for a source for the conception, however, outside Plotinus's own thought, it is impossible not to be struck by the resemblance to the Logos of Philo. The Philonian Logos, like that of Plotinus, is the principle of unity-in-diversity, of the separation and uniting of contraries in the material world.[1] It is the universal law, the principle of order in the world, distributing to each the lot appropriate to him.[2] These resemblances by themselves would not be so striking. They could be explained by the common philosophical heritage of the two thinkers, and especially by their dependence on the Stoic tradition.[3] What seems to bring Plotinus in these treatises very close to Philo is the fact that his Logos is, more than any other hypostasis in the *Enneads*, presented simply as an intermediary between the Divine and the material world. It has no other function except to be the instrument by which the order

[1] *Quis rer. divin. heres sit*, 130–40, 213; *De Plantat. Noë*, 5–10; *De Fuga*, I. 112; *Qu. in Exod.* II. 90, 118.

[2] *De Opif. Mundi*, 143.

[3] Cp. for Stoic influence on Philo Heinze, *Lehre vom Logos*, pp. 228 ff.; Aall, *Gesch. d. Logos-Idee*, I. 223. For the Stoic Logos as principle of separation and uniting, cp. S.V.F. I. 497 (Cleanthes).

of the Ideal world of Νοῦς is realized in the things of sense. In the same way the Logos of Philo is simply an intermediary between God and the material creation.[1] It may be possible to explain this as a coincidence, and to look for the origin of Plotinus's conception along the lines already suggested. We can regard his account of the Logos as simply designed to serve the immediate purposes of a theodicy, and not to be pressed too far. If, however, we are to look for any external source for the doctrine, it seems that the only resemblance to it in the work of any earlier thinker is to be found in Philo's description of his Logos.

I have given elsewhere[2] reasons for making comparatively little of the influence of Plato's *Laws* on the conception of the moral order in the world contained in these treatises. The great difference here between Plato and Plotinus is due to the entrance into Greek philosophy of the conception of a necessary, automatic world-order. Plato's God or gods in the *Laws* are primarily the guardians of the moral order.[3] The Logos is so only incidentally, as part of the working out of a universal order, moral indeed in a sense but entirely automatic and reflecting no conscious purpose or volition or choice between good and evil on the part of the higher powers. The difference is due to a development rather than a contradiction,[4] but it is a real one.

[1] *Quis rer. divin. heres sit*, 205; *De Somn.* II. 228; cp. Lebreton, vol. I, especially pp. 235–7.

[2] In an article, "The Gods in Plato, Plotinus, Epicurus", *Classical Quarterly*, vol. XXXII, July–October 1938.

[3] *Laws*, 905 D–907 B.

[4] Plotinus's idea of the universal order seems to be foreshadowed, though by no means fully expressed, in Plato's account of the divine government of the world, *Laws* 903 E–904 E.

CHAPTER VIII

CONCLUSION

WE have now enough information at our disposal to make possible a general survey of the structure of reality, according to Plotinus. At the head of his system stands a transcendent first principle, or ground of being and goodness, the One, which is ineffable and incomprehensible both to the discursive and the intuitive reason. This ineffability is represented by Plotinus in two ways. Either the One is ineffable as transcending our powers of thought or expression, as being more real than any being, better than any good which we can know or imagine, or it is ineffable as being unity-absolute to which no predicates can be applied for fear of involving it in multiplicity. The first way of thinking is that which predominates in the *Enneads*, because it is only by regarding it in this manner that the One can be brought into any relation to the rest of reality.

Below the One lie the two hypostases which are the universal correlatives of the whole range of human life, physical and intellectual. These are Νοῦς, Aristotle's Active Reason informed by and joined in a co-equal unity-in-diversity with the World of Ideas, themselves living and intelligent; and Soul, whose functions range from contemplation within the realm of Νοῦς to the information and direction of the material world. These hypostases are united to each other and to the One by a double link, a pair of contrary and complementary movements. The first is one of emanation or radiation of the lower from the higher, the second that of return in contemplation of the lower upon the higher. In the first of these movements the lower receives an indeterminate and potential existence, in the second it offers itself as matter to the higher as form, and so attains full reality.[1] The connections between Νοῦς and the One

[1] It is hardly necessary to say that there is no question here of change or succession in time. The hypostases and the relations between them are eternal and unchanging.

and Soul and Noῦς are described in exactly the same terms. In practice, however, the connection of Soul and Noῦς is generally much the closer of the two. Soul has its rightful home in the world of Noῦς and its highest activity is a sharing in that of Noῦς. On the other hand Plotinus usually speaks of the One as utterly transcending Noῦς, which can only apprehend it by leaving itself behind. He sometimes brings it within the range of human life by making the soul's supreme self-realization the realization of its identity with the One. There are, however, very few passages in which this is explicitly stated. As some of Plotinus's modern interpreters have seen, this way of thinking, if pushed to its logical conclusion, would destroy all possibility of a cosmology, or of any sort of philosophical thinking. All differences, all separate realities between which relations could be discerned, would be swallowed up in an infinite unity, inaccessible to reason (which could only operate in an illusory world of separation, of distinct things and persons), and only reached in the mystical union after all thought has ceased. This consideration cannot, however, form a basis for condemning Plotinus's philosophy wholesale as irrational and self-destructive, as Heinemann especially seems inclined to do. Plotinus usually speaks with the greatest restraint of the mystical union with the One, and surrounds it with many qualifications. He seems to think of it normally as a temporary unification in which all consciousness of difference is lost rather than a realization of a pre-existing identity.

The lowest stage in the cosmic order is the material universe, which lies within the sphere of soul. Plotinus's accounts of this lower universe and of its relation to the higher levels of being vary somewhat according to the point of view from which he is writing, and are not altogether reconcilable. Sometimes he concentrates his attention on the soul as it is in itself, sometimes on the material universe as an ensouled body or living organism, and sometimes on matter considered in isolation. In the first case he is chiefly concerned to make clear the distinction between the various stages of the life of soul, and to maintain its essential independence and separation from matter. In the second, the distinctions between the levels of soul fall into the background and the material universe is presented as a living whole, deriving its life and organic character from the soul which stretches unbroken through every part. When he is considering matter by itself Plotinus seems irresistibly drawn to regard it as the principle of evil; he insists too always, in opposition to Aristotle, that there can be no real union between matter and form. Even the lowest vestige of soul in body does not unite with matter to form the concrete material thing, but is externally superimposed upon it.

In spite of the obscurities caused by this variation in the point of view there are certain features in the account of soul and its working in the material universe which are found fairly constantly throughout the *Enneads*. There is always a tripartite division of soul, into the transcendent higher universal soul, the immanent but separate lower universal soul or nature, and the "vestiges of soul", the forms which give life and reality to material things. The lower soul is a true hypostasis produced by emanation. Occasionally the perceptive principle seems to occupy almost the position of another hypostasis. The individual souls are distinguished from the universal by their function. They are occupied with parts, not with the whole. The material universe which derives life and reality from this triplex soul is conceived as organic in a way which owes a good deal to Stoic philosophy and a good deal to contemporary magico-astrological ideas, and above all to the account of the visible universe in the *Timaeus*. Its organic character must, however, be qualified by the independence of soul which never really for Plotinus unites with body to form a single whole any more than form does with matter. The complex structure of soul, which alone in the material world is truly real, is superimposed on a substrate which always remains alien to it and outside it.

Two points of great importance for the understanding of Plotinus's philosophy are, first that the production of each lower stage of being from the higher is not the result of any conscious act on the part of the latter, but is a necessary, unconscious reflex of its primary activity of contemplation; and, second, that every level of real being, even the lowest, is good. Plotinus may speak of matter, which is absolute non-existence, as evil, but he is intensely anxious to demonstrate the complete goodness of the material world, the glorious image of its still more glorious archetype, the world of Νοῦς.

It can easily be seen from this summary that Plotinus in his account of the structure of reality is neither a pantheist nor a dualist, though both pantheistic and dualistic passages are to be found in the *Enneads*. Nor does he hold anything like the Judaeo-Christian doctrine of creation. He presents the universe as a static hierarchy of differing levels of life and reality. There is an unbroken continuity throughout from the highest to almost the lowest, from the One to the form in body, if not to the matter. Every stage of being is necessary to the perfection of the whole and the higher stages are eternal both as a whole and in all their parts. Even the material universe is eternal as a whole. Time is of little importance in the system of Plotinus. All the most important part of the life of the soul is lived outside time. No historical event could ever be for him of vital and decisive importance. This is one of the essential points of difference which separate him, and with him the whole Hellenic philosophical tradition, from Christian thought.

In all this Plotinus is thoroughly Greek, and in the direct line of succession from Plato and Aristotle. He has every right to call himself a Platonist, and his differences from his master are to a great extent due to the influence of the more developed thought of Aristotle. The influence on him of Stoic thought is perhaps less than has been generally supposed. It shows itself mainly in the general spirit and temper of his writing and in the terms which he uses rather than in his actual metaphysical doctrines. The point in his system where the influence is at its strongest is where he is dealing with the conception of the world as an organic whole and the ethical ideas which it involves. The Orientalizing tendencies of Plotinus's time have left comparatively few signs of their influence in the *Enneads*. They are most clearly apparent where he is dealing with the relations between the hypostases, in the theory of emanation. As for the influence of Oriental philosophies outside the Mediterranean world altogether, however attractive and to some extent enlightening it may be to draw parallels between them and the philosophy of Plotinus, there is not enough evidence to show that they had any effect upon him. Even the doctrine of the "infinite self" with its striking resemblance to Indian thought has, as I have tried to show, a probable origin in Peripatetic teaching about the Active Reason.

Plotinus's system is predominantly psychological. By this I do not mean to imply that he is a subjective idealist, but that the traditional Greek idea of the close correspondence of the macrocosm and the microcosm is the essential foundation of his system. He does not hold that man's mind has created the order of the universe which it observes. He does hold that man's mind and soul are part of a universal mind and soul which produce and vitalize the universe and that the structure of the universal ruling principle can be deduced from the study of the ruling principle in man. In this he follows the tradition of Plato and Aristotle, though he is more conscious of what he is doing than his predecessors and more elaborate and coherent in the working out of his thought. The realm of soul for Plotinus (using the word in Plato's sense, to include νοῦς) includes the whole of reality except the One, its transcendent source, and matter which falls outside the real world altogether. Nothing is real which is not also soul, and there is a stage of the universal soul to correspond to every level of human experience. The structure and divisions of reality are determined not so much by cosmological considerations as by the need to bring it into exact correspondence with the structure of the human soul and mind as determined by the Platonic-Aristotelian tradition and by Plotinus's own introspection. To a certain extent this heroic anthropomorphizing of the universe can be justified, and is essential to any philosophy which is not content to stop at a radical scepticism; and Plotinus is very careful to avoid any descent into the cruder sorts of anthropomorphism. There seem to be only two possibilities for the philosopher; either to admit that there is no universe at all, or that if there is it is inaccessible to our perceptions and intelligence; or else to hold that we are so far made in the universal image, and the universe is so far anthropomorphic, that it is controlled by a universal mind or soul. Plotinus's psychological anthropomorphism, however, goes a good deal beyond this necessary minimum. He can, I think, legitimately be criticized for elaborating his cosmology more than was rationally necessary in order to make it fit in with his views about the nature of the human soul and intellect.

I believe that the thought of Plotinus contains much that is of permanent philosophical and religious value. No adherent of the traditional European philosophy can regard the study of the *Enneads* as belonging to the "Wissenschaft des Nichtwissenswert". There do seem, however, to be certain extremely important points in the Plotinian system which lie open to serious and far-reaching objection. The criticisms which can be made fall under two heads, first the unnecessary multiplication of entities in the system and second the attempt to provide a comprehensible and coherent connection at points where the reason seems to show not a connection but a gulf, or at least a connection not comprehensible to the human intellect. Plotinus shares the common Hellenic fault of wishing to make reality too tidy, a fault which is after all only an exaggeration of a fundamental virtue, the desire to find a rational order in things that will make coherent thought about reality possible.

The conception of an Absolute, original reality, or ground of being, differing in the kind of its being from the relative and derived entities which it supports in existence, seems to be rationally well founded. There are many ways of arriving at it.[1] This is not a suitable place for a full exposition of the arguments, and a summary would be unsatisfactory and unconvincing. But it is of some importance, for the purpose of understanding the criticism of Plotinus which I am about to make, to be clear about the general principle on which they are founded. This is that the beings which we know are not self-sufficient or self-explanatory. Their being presents itself to our minds as relative and derived, and as requiring a supreme reality, being-in-itself and ground of the being of other things, to explain it. This absolute being, distinct from the being of particular things, obviously cannot be a "universal" or abstraction, for it is clear that if we attempt to abstract being from a being

[1] Mr Hardie puts forward some interesting suggestions on this point in the Additional Note to his *Study in Plato*, pp. 157–71.

it cannot be done, for nothing remains from which to abstract. The being of the Absolute must differ not only in degree but in kind from that of the relative and derived beings which we know. In this sense it can be said to be "beyond being". It is unknowable as it is in itself. We can only know *of* it, know that it must be there, through our knowledge of the beings which derive their reality from it. Parmenides was right when he maintained that Being-in-itself must be wholly other than the "beings" of our ordinary experience. Because there is no way in which Being as such can be limited or qualified it must be outside space and time, eternal, unchanging and undifferentiated. Where Parmenides went wrong was in maintaining (if he really did) the total unreality and illusoriness of relative and derived beings; for it is only through these latter that we can know of the Absolute. If we deny their reality, we are sawing off the branch we are sitting on.

The "positive" conception of the One in the *Enneads* is the nearest approach in Greek philosophy to this idea of the Absolute. The complications with which it is surrounded, however, have not so much rational justification. The first point which calls for attention is the very sharp separation between the One and Νοῦς. Many of the characteristics of the Absolute are common to the intelligible universe as a whole, the three great Hypostases including the transcendent Soul, as contrasted with the changeable, transitory and dependent existence of the material universe. This is particularly true of Νοῦς which, as we have seen, has always a tendency to become a duplicate of the "positive" conception of the One. If we read VI. 4 and 5, where the distinction between Νοῦς and the One falls very much into the background, with the traditional conception of Absolute Being in our minds which I have just outlined, we shall find Plotinus coming closer to it in these treatises than almost anywhere else in the *Enneads*. Nevertheless he reserves the distinctive attributes of transcendence and unknowability exclusively for the One. Further, Plotinus would criticize my account of the Absolute very sharply at one point. He would say that what I have described was rather the One-Being than the One and that another principle beyond it was necessary which was unity unpredicable, not only transcending all the beings we know but definitely and certainly not being and other than being. At this point the "positive" system, in which the One is the supreme principle of reality, meets and is affected by the "negative" or "mathematical logical" system, in which the One is Unity-Absolute. This provides one reason for Plotinus's maintaining of the distinction between the One and Νοῦς. Other reasons derive from the "psychological" aspect of his thought. Νοῦς represents the highest stage of purely human consciousness. We only reach the One by transcending ourselves. This can be expressed in a rather different way by saying that the world of Νοῦς corresponds to the highest stage of human knowledge of reality, which, if it is to be knowledge at all, must be knowledge of a unity-in-multiplicity. The One, which is bare unity, is beyond knowledge and can be reached only in the mystical union.

I have already dealt more fully with these distinctions between the One and Νοῦς in my first three chapters. My purpose in recapitulating them here is to enquire whether they have any rational justification. The "mathematical-logical" view of the One will surely be admitted by both modernist and traditionalist thinkers to belong to a world of archaic mathematics and exploded logical puzzles which can only be of historical interest for us. We may still have to take the historical Parmenides seriously, because he was the first to raise a question of vital importance to all philosophy; but there is no reason why we should take the Neo-Platonic interpretations of Plato's *Parmenides* seriously. The only form of the "negative theology" which seems to be of permanent value is that which I have called the "negative theology of positive transcendence", the "analogical" method. The statement that God or the Absolute is "not being" or "beyond being" only seems to have any meaning when it signifies "differing in kind from all the beings of which we have direct knowledge". In this sense it is, as we have seen, a necessary part of the conception of an Absolute.

I have already dealt with the "psychological" argument for the separation of Νοῦς and the One in the concluding section of my chapter on "The One and the Spiritual Life".[1] The conclusion

[1] Pp. 45–47.

which I there came to was that the mystical union and that clear knowledge which involves seeing the object known as a unity-in-multiplicity were not necessarily directed to different objects but might both be different ways of apprehending the same object. Further, it has become clear in our discussion of the doctrine of the Absolute that the attribution to It of Being, and hence of predicability and, in Plotinus's sense, of multiplicity does not necessarily mean that it is directly knowable to us. In fact, Absolute Being is as we have seen necessarily unknowable as it is in itself. In this way the transcendence of the One is saved even if it is identified with the One-Being.

There is still the larger question to be considered whether the "psychological" hypostases, Νοῦς and the transcendent Soul, are necessary to Plotinus's cosmology at all, or whether their functions can legitimately be attributed to the Absolute. To anyone who has assimilated certain points in the teaching of the *Enneads* it would seem that they can. There can certainly be no place in the mind of anyone who has studied Plotinus for the idea that the dignity of the Highest demands the intervention of intermediaries between it and the material universe. Nor does Plotinus fall into the error of supposing that transcendence means separation. The One and Νοῦς are most intimately omnipresent to all the lower levels of being just because they transcend them so utterly. Plotinus also teaches quite clearly that the governance of the lower calls for no sort of effort, change, disturbance, or application on the part of the higher, when we are dealing with omnipotent spiritual beings whose sway is co-extensive with the All. Their eternal inturned contemplation is not broken or perturbed by their secondary activity of creation or ruling. The too anthropomorphic pictures we are inclined to form of a rather fussy Providence struggling with a mass of small details, or alternatively of a God who is "too great" to bother about such little matters, are delusions based on a mistaken application to the higher world of our experience of the world of space and time and of the activities of finite beings. For all these reasons there seems no cause, other than a desire to cling blindly to the Platonic tradition, to place a transcendent Soul below the One-Being to form and rule the material universe. The functions attributed by Plotinus to his Three Hypostases can all be attributed to a single transcendent Being. To maintain the Plotinian hierarchy without the traditional reasons which led him to postulate it would be to multiply entities altogether without necessity and to hide the great amount of permanent value that there is in his description of it.

The position of the Ideas in this simplification of the system requires attention. One of the main functions of Νοῦς in Plotinus's scheme is to be the world of Ideas, the Archetype on which the universe of sense is modelled. It is difficult to see how the One can be the world of Ideas, even if it is identified with Absolute Being. It is doubtful, however, whether it is necessary to postulate a world of Ideas in the Plotinian sense, especially as they are not to be identified with the Forms of bodies, the element of permanent order and pattern in the material world which is the object of physical science. The finite, relative beings of this world must be regarded as in some sense "imitations", reflections on a different level of being of the One Absolute, and as in some unknowable manner "participating" in its being as the condition of their own existence. Further, this One-Being must be considered to be Mind in the same transcendent and analogical sense in which it is One and Good; and, being itself the primary object of its thought and having perfect self-knowledge it must in knowing itself know all its effects, all the relative and derived beings which it is capable of producing. This knowledge is of course eternal; it is the being of the Absolute; there is no separation between thought and object of thought, between actuality and activity. In this way we can still say that the archetypal, eternal world of Ideas is at least the symbol of a reality, of the eternal and all-inclusive being and knowledge of the Absolute. More than this we cannot concede to the doctrine.

Our examination of the validity of the system of Plotinus has left us with the conclusion that the part of it which is of the greatest permanent value is the "positive" doctrine of the One. His account of Νοῦς and Soul may be of the greatest value as an account of human states of consciousness, as a perfection and summing-up of the self-analysis of the great minds of the Hellenic philosophical tradition, but it does not seem possible to find a legitimate place for it in cosmology. There are of course innumerable details in the account which are most valuable when they are applied to the working of the Absolute; notably the doctrine of the immanent transcendence of the One-Being and in general Plotinus's very clear perception of the freedom of pure spirit from the limitations of space and time. The doctrine of the Three Hypostases, however, as a whole seems to be an unnecessary complication. With it of course goes the theory of emanation, which we have already seen to be unsatisfactory. Plato was wiser in refusing to define "participation". The relation between the Absolute and relative and derived beings must always remain mysterious because one term of it is inaccessible to our knowledge and because it is necessarily a unique relation about which we can form no general concept. The wise philosopher will be content to note that there is at this point a gulf or cleft in being and leave it at that.

Plotinus's account of the material universe will also require criticism and reconstruction if we are to see clearly the very large amount of it which is of permanent value. Here again Plotinus is often his own best critic. His insistence on the goodness of the sense-world, its worthiness of its maker and Father and his denial, at his best, of any real causality to "matter" make particularly unnecessary and inappropriate his shrinking from the admission of any real coalescence between matter and form. The "layering" tendency, the rather nervous desire to interpolate as many stages of being as possible between the higher life of the soul and the material universe, is the weakest part of his account of the latter. If we remember how clearly he teaches that the "separation" from the body which the philosopher should desire is not a physical one, but depends on the direction of his intellect and will, we shall not feel tempted to follow him in these rather clumsy attempts to increase the distance between soul and matter in his cosmology.

One of the features of Plotinus's cosmology for which he seems to me most worthy of praise is his determined assertion at the same time of the reality of human free will and of the universal order. In this of course he follows the best Hellenic tradition: but he sees the real importance and difficulty of combining the two conceptions far more clearly than his predecessors. He does not overcome the difficulties involved; what philosopher ever has overcome them completely? But he at least presents a picture of the world in which the idea of morality has some meaning, in which it is possible to believe both in a moral law and in some measure of personal responsibility for keeping it.

This statement of my personal view of the validity of Plotinus's philosophical system may seem to have left very little of it standing. It is, however, because I believe so firmly in the great and permanent value of the philosophy of Plotinus that I have been impelled to make it. Plotinus is not only the most vital connecting link in the history of European philosophy, as being the philosopher in whom the Hellenic tradition in full development and maturity was brought into touch with the beginnings of Christian philosophy. He is also one of the few ancient philosophers whom we can still honour, though not uncritically, as a master, and not simply study as a historical curiosity.

INDEX OF NAMES

REGISTER OF PASSAGES FROM THE ENNEADS REFERRED TO

Where no chapter number is given the reference is to the treatise as a whole.

Printed in the United States
By Bookmasters